SOTHIS PRESS

Sothis Press aims to completely reimagine the public domain book with an emphasis on universal access to captivatingly designed print editions. We believe that technology will enable every single book ever published to be perpetually accessible in beautiful print form. Sothis is beauty in ubiquity.

www.sothis.press
1 Waterhouse Square, London, ECIN 2ST

Labour and Housing at Port Sunlight

W. L. George

SOTHIS PRESS

ISBN 978-1-0368-0574-6

This edition is published by
Sothis Press © 2023. The company
is registered in England and Wales.
The Company Number is 14900389.

PORT SUNLIGHT: GEOGRAPHICAL POSITION. [*Frontispiece.*

LABOUR AND HOUSING
AT
PORT SUNLIGHT

BY

W. L. GEORGE

AUTHOR OF

"ENGINES OF SOCIAL PROGRESS," "FRANCE IN THE TWENTIETH CENTURY," ETC.

LONDON: ALSTON RIVERS, LIMITED
BROOKE STREET, HOLBORN BARS
1909

PRINTED BY
WILLIAM CLOWES AND SONS, LIMITED,
LONDON AND BECCLES.

PREFACE

THE writing of a comparatively lengthy treatise upon so complicated a theme as Port Sunlight would have been impossible without the co-operation of all those who fill special positions in the Village, for they alone are in possession of detailed information. I am glad to bear witness to the generous and whole-hearted manner in which all the officials of the Works and the members of the committees of the institutions placed their knowledge at my disposal. It would be pleasant to be able to thank them all, and to let them know that without their help this book could not have been exhaustive, but that they are too numerous will easily be gathered from the following rough list of interviews which I had whilst at Port Sunlight:—

Working men and women . . .	31
Clerks	11
Foremen and officials	9
Employees of institutions and others .	36
	87

Among the "others" are the hospital, public-house,

and church staffs, etc. I should, however, like to mention two persons, the value of whose help I cannot overrate. One is Miss H. A. Carson, B.A., who has kindly undertaken the arduous task of revising and correcting the subject-matter of this book and who has placed at my disposal much valuable information concerning education, etc. The other is Mr. W. H. Williams, the Social Secretary of Port Sunlight, thanks to whom I was able to collect abundant notes. He has been unsparing in his pains both during and since my stay in the Village; it is not too much to say that without him the book could not have been written at all.

W. L. G.

CONTENTS

ILLUSTRATIONS

LABOUR AND HOUSING AT PORT SUNLIGHT

CHAPTER I

HISTORICAL

AMONGST the many significant developments of the last twenty years, the promotion of social schemes is perhaps the most striking proof that the nature of man has rapidly been changing and that the twentieth century will witness many innovations that would have appeared Utopian to our older schools of individualists. The movement inaugurated by the "good" Lord Shaftesbury has gained such momentum that we have begun to look upon the study of industrial betterment as an exact science, upon the putting in practice of the newly evolved principles as a duty. Thus it is not surprising to see a reaction setting in against the iron laws that governed industry during the early Victorian era, a reaction in favour of good housing and fair treatment for the workers; we have at last begun to look upon the worker as something more than a dividend-earning machine, to recognize his rights as a man and a brother. Whether this be a direct result of the successive Reform Bills which have placed power in the hands of the people, and of compulsory free education tending to make them fit to use this power, or whether our new outlook is due to the tardy awakening of the national conscience, we need not attempt to decide.

The practical social worker concerns himself little with motives and origins; for him there is only one question to be put: Is this good for the people? For him there is no tainted money; for him no instalment of justice, no token of good-will is so small that he cannot accept it. He knows naught but love of the people and, burning with their wrongs, he will willingly accept any sacrifice of dignity, even forego more or less illusory privileges of freedom, if such abnegation can become the means of regenerating his fellows; for he knows well that ultimately mankind will reassert itself and, strengthened and purified, triumphantly attain that which is its own by right.

The modern social spirit is a spirit of expediency; in no previous period of history has compromise reigned supreme as it does nowadays in Great Britain, and never has a force worked so potently for the public good. I do not seek to cast a slur upon extremists, whether sunk in crude individualism or floating in the ether of "might be"; they are valuable and indeed, essential, components of the body politic, which they leaven and invigorate; but, superior as they may be to the invertebrate "average," their works are not direct, not concrete. The active social worker has a composite personality, for he belongs by temperament to the section of extreme dreamers and yet has enough of the "average" characteristics to limit in some degree the flights of his enthusiasm. These three—

the capitalistic octopus, the Laodicean average man, and the social reformer whose life is a dream of ideals—are the basic types; from the highest to the lowest the gradation is infinite, but the truly useful social worker is the man of the central type, influenced by thoughts of higher things. Such a man will compromise, and thus only can he hope to succeed.

The ancient democrats and revolutionaries, particularly those of the seventeenth and early nineteenth centuries, are examples of this peculiar type, rich in common sense as in ideals, and able, like Mortensgore, "to will only that to which they know they can attain." Our modern social workers are of a different stamp, for their efforts are now directed less against what we call political than against "social" evils; their aim is to heal the diseases of our economic system rather than to reconstruct it in its entirety; thus they strive less for a democratic franchise, for a representative Second Chamber, than for such reforms as improved housing and more equitable land tenure. They seek to minimize existing evils in the hope of ultimately uprooting them, when at last the nature of man will be born again and he will come into his birthright.

It is to this new spirit, therefore, that we can trace the numerous schemes which have been promoted for the benefit of the people. These schemes vary with the temperament of their originators; some are entirely philanthropic, others severely business-like, but even the latter are tinged with good-will. It would be difficult to classify these efforts, but they all tend in the same direction, whether they be those of a Peabody or an Iveagh, a Cadbury or a Howard, a Livesey or a Lever. For the social student it matters little to what party these men belong, however distasteful he may find their political views ; it matters even little whether their works were originally intended to enslave the people yet further, to warp their minds or destroy their power of combination ; all he needs to know is whether the balance of betterment is in their favour or not ; if it be favourable (and any nefarious plans have miscarried) then he will not hesitate to give them his approval and his most loyal support.

The schemes referred to are representative of the three classes of social work. The Peabody Fund, the Guinness Trust, and Bournville Village are philanthropic in their origin, for their promoters demanded no return for their outlay and abandoned, in favour of further extension, any profits that might eventually accrue to them ; Garden City stands midway between altruism and egoism, for it limits the profits of its supporters and makes over eventual credit balances to the people ; the South Metropolitan Gas Company * and Port Sunlight are instances of the third class, namely, purely business-like transactions informed by good-will. As these differences are fully dealt with in another chapter it is unnecessary to say more about them here ; it is enough to note at the outset that Port Sunlight belongs to the "business" group, and then to show that such classification is correct.

Philanthropy pure and simple is often required to lead the way in social effort, to arouse public opinion and sow in men's minds the seed from which progress will spring ; to this, however, its function is limited and, if it enter the executive ranks of social work, it is

* The late Sir George Livesey's scheme.

INSANITARY PROPERTY STANDING FORMERLY ON THE SITE OF THE VILLAGE.

[*To face p.* 4.

likely to do more harm than good, to create as many unfortunates as it relieves, and thus to perpetuate the very evils against which it struggles. Of course there are many cases in which philanthropy alone can act, such as the immediate relief of unemployment, the immediate rescue of the hungry child, but the adjective "immediate" explains that philanthropic action is only a makeshift, and that we can build upon it nothing real and permanent. No *social* scheme is worthy of the name unless it can be made to pay its way; we do not want to see our co-operative societies, housing systems, or land settlements turned into profit-earning organizations, but they must be self-supporting. Groups of this kind can justify their existence only by subsisting independently of outside help, otherwise they are hardly worth preserving.

Port Sunlight, as has already been said, is not a philanthropic venture, nor is it a dividend-earning concern; it is an attempt to establish a good understanding between the warring forces of Capital and Labour, for the greater benefit of both; in the words of the founder, "to Socialize and Christianize business relations and get back again in the office, factory, and workshop to that close family brotherhood that existed in the good old days of hand labour." *

Such an aim reveals a measure of idealism, and this alone entitles Port Sunlight to a place among social schemes, however commercial its basis may be; neither ideals nor business principles have been lost sight of; both in fact were good fairies invited to bless by their presence the birth of the Village.

* Paper by Mr. W. H. Lever, in the *Birkenhead News*, November 24, 1900.

THE ORIGIN OF PORT SUNLIGHT.—Port Sunlight is an infant city, for it attains its majority only in March of next year, the first sod having been cut in March, 1888; strictly speaking, the Village came into existence only at the end of 1889, so that it does not at present date back much further than nineteen years. So settled and organized is the little community that this is hardly apparent to the visitor, except when he crosses the large open spaces enclosed in the estate, which are clearly still in process of development. The origin of the Village must be sought in the extension of the Works, and in this, at the inception, we already find the link between the industry and the workers which, down to the present day, has never been broken. When, in 1887, the Warrington soap works became cramped for space, Messrs. Lever Brothers decided to remove to some distant site where their industry could expand; at that time the Village was not formally planned: the main object of the removal was to obtain cheap land and enough of it. The site was chosen near the Mersey, a little south of New Ferry, on the banks of an inlet known as Bromborough Pool; it extended over about fifty-six acres and was acquired at the comparatively cheap rate of £200 per acre, which is not surprising to those who remember the estate as it then was.

Anything more unprepossessing than this site can hardly be imagined. It was mostly but a few feet above high-water level, and liable at any time to be flooded by high tides, and thus to become undistinguishable from the muddy foreshores of the Mersey. Moreover, an arm of Bromborough Pool spread in various directions through the Village, filling the ravines with ooze and slime ; a few houses, or rather shanties, were scattered on the higher portions, whose condition as regards sanitation can easily be conjectured. It was land suitable for a dock, but it did not, at first sight, seem fitted for human settlement. Since 1887, however, twenty years of work have so changed the face of the estate as to make it unrecognizable ; apart from building operations, the very topography has been recast. Not only has the area been increased to two hundred and twenty-one acres, of which some one hundred and thirty are now devoted to the Village, but a certain amount of land has been reclaimed. I can recollect the time (eight years ago) when a sheet of stagnant water filled the Bromborough Pool dell. It has been dammed and surrounded with smiling houses, so that the numerous hollows in the Village are free from the menace of floods. These, too, are being drained and half filled up ; some have already been partly planted with trees, while the rest are being treated in the same manner ; a radical change has taken place, and the swamps that once disgraced the neighbourhood are now almost entirely transformed from centres of infection into grass-grown open spaces and playing fields.

At the present time Port Sunlight extends over a slope rising gently from Bromborough Pool, an arm of the Mersey, to about forty feet above it ; at the water's edge are the Works with their dock, very few houses being nearer the Pool than three hundred yards. This rising ground is broken by the hollows marked on the map, at present three in number. The largest, over which Victoria Bridge has been built, was once directly connected with, and practically a portion of, Bromborough Pool, but it is now cut off by a dam, and is being filled up; it is already partly occupied by the rifle-range, and the remainder will never be built on, but will be used either as a public garden or as allotment land. The second dell, which formerly communicated with the first, has been turned into a park, which already boasts fine trees and is partly occupied by the auditorium. The third hollow lies towards the north-west; this, too, has been drained, and is now an excellent playing field with wooded banks. It is indeed characteristic of Port Sunlight that rusticity has everywhere been preserved; the builder has almost invariably respected the trees, which are numerous and healthy; so great was his regard for them that, in several places, they have even been allowed to encroach upon the footway, thus adding to the rural effect.

It will be gathered from all this that the transformation has been considerable; indeed, it is not too much to say that the bulk of the estate consists of land that has been reclaimed for human inhabitation, for an insanitary area has within twenty years been transformed into a flourishing and healthy village, very green and English in its aspect, and clean as the proverbial Dutch town.

PROSPERITY-SHARING BASIS.—Before, however, describing the Village in detail, it is necessary to obtain an idea of the basis of the scheme which it represents. As has already been said, the necessities of the business necessitated its removal from Warrington, and it was only some time afterwards that the idea which was forming in the mind of the founder

VICTORIA BRIDGE.

[*To face p.* 8.

began to take shape; whether future developments on such a scale were anticipated may be doubted, but it is safe to say that prosperous works, and, side by side with them, an industrial village, were already aimed at. It was only later that the ideals took definite shape, and that the improvement and extension of Port Sunlight became comparable to profit-sharing. At the present time, however, the Village is emphatically a profit-sharing scheme on improved lines, *i.e.* Prosperity-sharing.

The early Victorian idea of profit-sharing is probably by this time relegated to the limbo of theory; in principle, the idea of a participation by the employees in the profits of an enterprise is exceedingly attractive. It suggests close co-operation between master and workman, where each man would strive for the benefit of all, would be nerved to do his best, and thus to rise above the level of wage-earning slavery up to that of industrial partnership. In the years that preceded the Factory Acts, when unrestrained commercial tyranny prevailed in every trade and sweating was rather the rule than the exception, profit-sharing appeared as an ideal application in a minor degree of the altruistic doctrines of Fourier and of Owen; thus it is not surprising that some social students should still cling to the old system, however it may have become discredited by actual practice. It must, of course, be understood, that by "old" theory is meant a distribution *in cash* among the workers of a portion of the profits.

OBJECTIONS TO PROFIT-SHARING.—There is no good to be said in the light of experience for profit-sharing pure and simple. In the first place, it is financially unsound, for the workers are allowed to participate in profits, but are not called upon to contribute to losses. Thus their share becomes a dole, and it is clear that, pleasant as it may be, the game of "heads I win, tails you lose," is not healthy for the winner; such a system is demoralizing to the worker, because his partnership is partial, so much so that he is a partner only in name, since, though he will thankfully accept a gift, he does not run any risk. It is, of course, absurd to suggest that the worker could accept reciprocal partnership if it were offered; as a rule, his only capital are his intelligence and his physical powers; he has but small reserves of cash, so small as to nullify their value in businesses that rest on credit. Modified social conditions might make this intimate connection possible; we are not, however, concerned now with eventual conditions (under which, by the way, it is conceivable that modern industry itself would be run on different lines), but with the present state of things.

The worker cannot become a full partner because of his lack of capital; but even if he were eligible, it would be folly for him to accept the position. As it is, he depends far too much on the prosperity of the undertaking that employs him. In an industrial crisis he is the first to suffer, for it brings at once short time, wage reductions, and dismissals. Capital can bear a crisis, for its reserves enable it to hold out until a glutted market has been cleared or credit re-established in the country; the position of the worker, on the other hand, is that he must find employment under pain of starvation, and his task becomes all the harder when bad times set in. Under the circumstances, can any one seriously suggest that the worker should bind himself to participate in losses during the lean years, in losses which would speedily sweep away his savings, leaving him at last bereft not only of his employment in the face of a dwindling demand for labour, but of the small capital that would have enabled him to keep the wolf from the door until conditions had improved? It does not do for a capitalist to place all his eggs in one basket; it is an elementary principle of finance that a banker must re-insure himself by spreading his investments over several countries and various ventures, so as not to find his funds suddenly tied up when demands upon them fall due; the worker must follow his example, and his precarious financial position must make him still more cautious than his employer. He must resolutely divorce his savings from his employment, so that the first may remain if the second fail him, and *vice versâ*.

Whether the worker be a full partner or not, there are yet graver objections to profit-sharing. As yet, partial partnership, *i.e.* participation in profits and not in losses, has alone been tried. A practical difficulty arises at once: how are the workers to determine what their participation should be if they are not allowed to know the amount of the total profits? It is, of course, impossible to allow the mass of workers to inspect the books, for the door would then be opened to every form of commercial *espionage*, and, besides, in the majority of cases, the books of an important undertaking can be understood by none but a skilled accountant. Thus, as regards divisible profit, the workers must take the masters' word and, as it is unfortunately too true that most men consider another's gain as their own loss, there is always reasonable ground for suspicion. The worker is inclined to think that his employer's object is to extract from him a maximum of work in exchange for a minimum of pay, and more often than not he is right; even a profit-sharing scheme does not do away with his suspicions, for he has learned by bitter experience that benevolence may be utilized for the mercenary purposes of his taskmaster.

Profit-sharing thus stultifies itself. Instead of fostering good feeling and co-operation between employer and employee, it tends to destroy any bond of kindliness that may already exist, by sowing the seeds of distrust. These seeds once sown, the advantages of profit-sharing vanish; the object of its introduction can only be an improvement in the quality and the quantity of the work produced, neither of which results is likely to follow when the worker labours under either a real, or a mistaken, sense of injury. In fact, it is directly conducive to trade disputes, given that the latter are as often traceable to mental as to material causes.

In limited companies, where the accounts are published and audited by qualified accountants, this particular difficulty in great part vanishes, but even if we set it aside in these cases (which leaves private firms where they were) further difficulties at once arise.

Profits are variable quantities and are largely influenced by the more or less conservative policy of the managers; should the latter see fit, for instance, to set aside a large sum for the purpose of creating a reserve, profits may for some years be reduced to a low figure, in fact, to vanishing point. This is often a wise precaution from the capitalist's point of view, and he can afford to take it, as he does not depend entirely on the profits of a single undertaking; he knows, moreover, that he will eventually reap enhanced benefits from prudent administration. But meanwhile, what of the worker? His employment is not secured him; he may have been for many years a faithful servant of the undertaking and find his services dispensed with at a week's notice. Thus his interest is to receive at once as great a proportion of the profits as possible; in fact, his interest is antagonistic to that of his employer, so that again more scope is given for dissension which inevitably reacts on the quality of the work.

PROFIT-SHARING LIMITS ENTERPRISE.—Having found the employer and the employee in conflict as regards matters of prudence, we now find them in conflict as regards enterprise. A growing business requires working capital, and it is not always possible or desirable to raise this by loan, or to create new shares; under such circumstances it is natural to use a portion of the profits for the purpose of, say, increasing the plant, establishing foreign agencies, etc. This is almost certain to happen in a rapidly growing business, and valuable opportunities of expansion may be wasted if they are not at once seized; this the enterprising capitalist will of course do, given his favourable position as regards the deferring of profits, but once more his interests are in direct conflict with those of the workers, for the same reasons as those given above with reference to measures of prudence. It may be said, on the whole, that any deflection of profits must be distasteful to the wage-earner, and that there exists no more efficacious means of creating difficulties between Capital and Labour. Apart, however, from these potential causes of disunion, a profit-sharing system of this elementary type, even if it works perfectly smoothly and yields satisfactory returns both to employer and employee, is still open to grave objections; if the profit-sharing consists of yearly or half-yearly doles it may seem perfectly successful and yet do the worker a great deal of harm. Profits are essentially varying quantities, and in most businesses they rise for a given number of years, attain a maximum, and then for some years decline, after which they again begin to rise. Apart from businesses in which profits increase slowly but regularly and without set-backs, the net yield of undertakings fluctuates according to the conditions of trade in the country; our system of production makes for a regular succession of gluts and shortages, which result in crises during which profits vary to a considerable extent: this is one of its most notable weaknesses and forms a serious count in the Socialist indictment. If, therefore, a fixed fraction of these profits is set aside for the workers, their annual bonus will fluctuate; if the worker were to look upon this bonus as an addition to capital this fluctuation, apart from the discontent it would create, would not matter very much, but it is notorious that he looks upon it as income and spends it in the same way as his wages. Thus, fluctuating bonuses mean, in reality, fluctuating wages, and I do not suppose that any one will consider this a healthy condition of affairs. During the good years the worker acquires habits of extravagance;

the more slowly profits increase, the greater is the harm done; if a man receives, say, £5 in one year, and £10 the next, he will perhaps set aside a portion of the increase; but if he receives £5 the first year, £6 the next, £7 for the third, and so on, he will feel the increases so little that he will spend his bonuses without a thought. Having acquired these habits, and increased his expenditure by, say, 10 per cent.,* he experiences considerable discomfort when the bad years that must inevitably follow begin to make themselves felt, and if he has made a practice of using his bonus for his pleasures, he may feel the pressure more acutely than if the necessaries of life were menaced.

PAST EXPERIMENTS IN PROFIT-SHARING.—Generally speaking, large yearly or half-yearly doles make for drunkenness and extravagance, and very rarely for thrift; other systems partaking of the same nature are often successful, but for profit-sharing pure and simple little good can be said. The truth of the statement is demonstrated by the history of the system: the facts that follow show it to have hitherto been a failure. Profit-sharing was originally introduced into this country by Lord Wallscourt, about 1830, on a hundred-acre farm; he expressed himself satisfied, but it is suggestive to note that all he congratulated himself upon was being able to leave his farm safely for a year at a time.† His scheme appears to have resulted in his running his farm without much trouble; whether it paid is another question, and the

* This is not an abnormal figure in profit-sharing schemes.

† Report by D. F. Schloss, to the Board of Trade, on profit-sharing (1894).

system certainly did not survive him. Lord Wallscourt's experiment yields in interest to the first important venture of this nature, that of Mr. Leclaire, in Paris, in 1842. The history of Leclaire is well known, and he well deserves the title of "father" of profit-sharing, even though he may have been forestalled by Lord Wallscourt, and by the economist Babbage in 1833. Leclaire organized his house-painting and decorating business on a profit-sharing basis, and ran it successfully for thirty-two years, during which the participation of his employees increased considerably; after his death, however, the policy of the undertaking (which was then placed on a basis of equal shares to workers and to capital) was altered, and profits were inflated apparently to the detriment of the turnover; thus, ten years after the death of Leclaire, the workers were receiving nearly three times as large a bonus as during the last year of his life, after which the business declined.

The Leclaire experiment was, to my mind, the triumph of an able and masterful business man, who would have succeeded under any circumstances; his character, which was remarkable for energy and initiative, fitted him for the position of leader, but without him, as is too often the case in social schemes, the undertaking could no longer hold its own. In order, however, not to lay too much stress upon a single experiment, it is useful to quote some facts which are vouched for by the Eleventh Abstract of Labour Statistics of the United Kingdom, issued in 1907. We find in this publication that in this country, up to the middle of 1906, 196 firms had initiated profit-sharing schemes, so that we have here an adequate basis for study, comprising, as it does, nearly 200 firms, by which are affected about 150,000 workers, and extending over some 77 years (1829–1906).

On the 30th of June, 1906, out of these 196 firms, no fewer than 122 had abandoned the system, and 14 yielded no particulars, leaving 60 in which profit-sharing was known to exist. Therefore, two out of three schemes, roughly speaking, had failed for various reasons; these 60 firms employed 47,317 workers, and it is at once apparent that profit-sharing cannot have demonstrated its commercial value, if, after 77 years of experiment, less than 50,000 workers were affected by it. Over half the employees were in engineering and ship-building yards, where a modicum of success would seem to have been attained, if we did not at the same time note that, by the middle of 1906, out of 18 schemes which had been established in this class of undertaking, 12 had failed.

It must not be thought that the bonuses were small; the Labour Abstract states that (in 1905) the mean bonus *in all cases* was 5½ per cent., and that the average bonus in those firms where one was actually paid was over 7 per cent. of the wages. Yet 122 firms out of 196 had abandoned the system, and it behoves us to inquire into the reasons. In 31 cases we find that the employers were dissatisfied with results, which shows that profit-sharing is not such "good business" as its strenuous advocates make out; in 20 cases, losses showed still more clearly that profit-sharing was not commercial, and in 26 cases the undertaking was dissolved, liquidated, or found its profits reduced. Thus, altogether, in 77 cases out of 122, the employer found that it was not to his advantage to continue the system; in 13 cases, on the other hand, the employees became dissatisfied or remained apathetic; the remaining 32 cases cannot be traced precisely to discontent on either side. On the whole, therefore, the employer had more reason to complain than the employee, but this is immaterial, for profit-sharing could justify itself in our present economic system only by enhancing the profits of both parties. This, except in a few cases, it has clearly not done.

CASE FOR PROSPERITY-SHARING.—I have dilated upon this subject, not only because attacks were made on these views, which I expressed in another volume,* but chiefly because the failure of profit-sharing pure and simple leads up to the alternative known as "prosperity-sharing." I do not know that this system is in vogue anywhere except in Port Sunlight, and it cannot be denied that there it works extremely well. In a limited sense it is profit-sharing, for a portion of the profits of the business is set aside for its purposes, but in a limited sense only. The financial basis of the scheme is fully set forth in another chapter, and for the present it is enough to say that the workers' share, instead of being paid out to them individually, is looked upon as being earned collectively, and becomes the property of the community. Instead of declaring that a certain proportion of his wages shall be paid to each worker in cash, over and above the agreed rate, the total wages earned are looked upon as a single whole, and the claim of the workers upon the profits is satisfied by a lump sum; this amount is used for the purpose of keeping up the

* "Engines of Social Progress" (1907).

Village and its institutions, as will be shown further on, when we come to deal with the finances of Port Sunlight.

Instead, therefore, of the worker being subjected to the demoralizing influence of irregular bonuses, he is given the opportunity of occupying a good house at a low rate in pleasant surroundings, and of taking part in an elevating communal life. The scheme is not without its shortcomings, particularly as regards those who cannot be accommodated in the Village, and who thus receive no benefit; also in the case of those who, being thrifty, require no protection against themselves, and would gladly receive a cash bonus instead of benefiting by ideal surroundings. Since, however, so little that is good can be said for profit-sharing pure and simple, and seeing that health, morality, and education are left practically untouched by more elaborate systems, such as that of the South Metropolitan Gas Company, it may reasonably be said that there is a *primâ facie* case for Port Sunlight. The object, therefore, of the following chapters is to show how this "prosperity-sharing" scheme is administered, how it affects the worker, his wife, and his child, and how it compares in both these respects with schemes which are of the same nature, but are conducted on different lines.

CHAPTER II

THE WORKS: HYGIENE AND SAFETY

POTENT as may be the influence of ideal housing, much of the work attempted in that direction would be sterile if the factory were not at the same time brought up to a high level of cleanliness, order, and safety. Even if the worker were well housed he would not easily shake off the effects of a long day's work in insanitary premises; indeed, it is not certain that ideal conditions are not more important in the factory than in the home. Industrial labour, in these days of machinery, is not, as a rule, so intellectual as to demand concentration upon the task; at any rate, it leaves time for the formation of impression—a process ever at work for good or evil. Thus it is important, not only that the worker's life and limbs should be protected, and that the workshop should satisfy a benign factory inspector, but that it should be spacious, well ventilated, and, as far as possible, beautiful.

The influence of the factory on the home is comparable with the influence of the master on the man; few will deny that a just and courageous employer can do much by force of example to lead his men into the paths of morality and rectitude: is it not likely, then, that continuous and conscious effort in the direction of cleanliness and simplicity will impel the worker to imitation in his home? The influence of beauty is subtle; at Port Sunlight there is enough evidence of fair dealing to justify a belief, by analogy, that, in the long run, beauty also will make its presence felt. Imitation is so normal a phenomenon and lies at the root of so many changes for the better, or the worse, that example cannot be overrated as regards the planning and the government of a factory.

It is certain that the grimy, unhealthy works, with which we are too familiar, react unfavourably upon the employees; it is, at any rate, singular that the latter are too often equally grimy and unhealthy, whereas from the gates of Port Sunlight emerges a crowd of cheerful and cleanly workers. A subtle sense of fitness pervades the atmosphere; where the workshops are foul and evil smelling, natural carelessness asserts itself, and we find the workers slatternly in body and slothful in mind; conversely, where conditions are good, men and women are encouraged or shamed by their surroundings, and unconsciously raise their tone to the prevailing level of cleanliness and order.

It is interesting to note, in this connection, evidence collected on the spot; soapworks are notoriously unsavoury places, and their existence is usually suspected by the visitor for some time before he sees them. This is not the case at Port Sunlight, as any one who has lived there can testify; indeed, the obnoxious part of the process seems to be confined to a single room, and even there it is not beyond endurance. Cleanliness is the secret, and I was told by foremen who had been employed in other works that this seemed to influence in a remarkable manner the spirit of the worker, who was not only more diligent and generally efficient, but more cheerful and open in mind. This is a solid asset, both financial and moral; but it does not come as a surprise upon the visitor when once he has been over the Works.

DISTINGUISHING FEATURES.—Apart from social aspects, the Port Sunlight Works are an industrial monument; the very fact that they extend over some ninety acres would be enough to justify such a statement; but there are many features that distinguish them from the ordinary factory. The first and general impression is, of course, one of size, and the visitor, hurrying from workshop to wharf, from office to railway siding, is bewildered by the variety and the complexity of the processes, by the innumerable ramifications of a business that involves no less than seventy trades. By degrees, however, he realizes how definite is the plan of operations, and how methodically the Works themselves have been organized for efficient operating; from the apparent chaos of industrialism emerges the understanding of the system; but wonder does not decrease with familiarity. Be that as it may, the first thing that strikes the social student is the fact that the Works have, as far as possible, been separated from the Village. They occupy the southern corner of the estate, which is also one of its lowest points, and interpose a severe, but not inharmonious, structure between the houses and the dock; this is an important feature, both sanitary and æsthetic. Space has not been spared, for roads varying in width between forty and one hundred and twenty feet separate the various blocks, so that air and light can penetrate freely on all sides. Thus, not only does the Factory not poison the district, but it also fosters good work and good spirits.

It would be too much to say that the Works are a thing of beauty. The factory that is an ornament to the neighbourhood has yet to be built by some disciple of William Morris; but there is in the Port Sunlight Works a severe solidity which is not unpleasing to the eye. From this particular point of view the offices are perhaps more interesting than the Works, owing partly to their being faced with white stone and surmounted by a colonnade, but more especially because they are single storied and lighted by enormous windows not less than ten feet high. This worship of sunshine (I had almost said sunlight) is characteristic of every building in the Village, and the impression is strengthened when we enter the offices and find that the entire roof is glazed. These are remarkable workrooms, for their height varies between twenty-five and thirty feet—an unusual feature, as visits to most city offices will demonstrate. The interior is superior to the exterior owing to the long graceful lines of the building; moreover, some care has been expended in making these offices pleasant. The floors are mosaic, the walls white or distempered a soft shade of green; near the roof are placed at intervals groups of flags of all nations, the effect of which is certainly pleasing. These form practically the only decoration; I do not know whether the organizers aimed at simplicity; if not, an opportunity is perhaps being wasted. The value of pictures and flowers is well known, and the broad expanse of wall could probably be made use of to good effect, as has been done in other factories.

The same applies to the exterior, where little gardens have been laid out and might well be extended, for here again there are great opportunities, as has been shown in many American and a few British factories. The Clements Manufacturing Company, in Massachusetts, for instance, has trained creepers to cover entirely the sides and roofs of its coalsheds; the Cadbury Works at Bournville are entered through a small park; Le Creusot, in central France, is practically "a factory in a garden." However, though further use might be made of much of the space between the blocks at Port Sunlight Works, it would be unfair to cavil at the efforts that have certainly been made towards decoration.

These remarks apply to the workshops as well as to the offices, for they also are almost invariably single storied, lofty, and well lighted; the floors are wood blocks, a fact which may appear unimportant to those who have not to stand on a cold floor for eight hours a day, winter and summer. These floors are cleaned weekly and, in some departments, daily; they are all, at any rate, swept and swabbed every day; it is lamentable to think that the state of our factories is still such as to make this worth mentioning. It is neither desirable nor possible here to describe in detail all the departments—sorting, pan-room, refinery, laboratory, box-making, glueing, packing, printing, ink-grinding, etc.; an adequate idea of the processes can only be gained by a personal inspection, an inspection, by the way, which is facilitated by the fact that galleries run round departments, some seven or eight feet above the floor; these galleries have, I believe, been built especially for visitors.

MEDICAL INSPECTION AND HEALTH PRESERVATION.—Apart from the processes themselves, one of the striking features of Port Sunlight is the care that has been expended in promoting the well-being of the employees and ensuring their immunity from accident. The excellent rule of medical examination is extensively applied, and too much can hardly be said on this subject. It is highly desirable that this examination should be made compulsory by law, for there are a certain number among the men, and a still larger proportion among the women and girls, who are too weakly in constitution to endure certain classes of work; we need a considerable increase in our staff of factory inspectors,* but we also require a new class, the medical factory inspectors, whose province it would be to certify not the premises, but the workers; such an inspection should, of course, be combined with facilities for treatment if necessary, coupled with maintenance, which should not be considered as outdoor relief. In the present state of things, however, an employer is free to engage whomsoever he chooses, for any purpose he chooses, without being compelled to consider whether this engagement is not the worker's death-warrant, or, a still more serious matter, whether his association with his fellows may not be fraught for them with grave dangers of infection;

* Mr. L. G. Chiozza Money, in "Riches and Poverty," shows that "each inspector has to deal, on an average, with one thousand six hundred and seventy-seven workplaces," so that each of these cannot reasonably be inspected more often than once every two and a-half years! (The calculation is mine.—W. L. G.)

consumption is a case in point, for it is slow in growth, and not easily detected. Messrs. Lever Brothers have, however, provided as far as possible against these contingencies. Every one of their employees is medically examined within one month of engagement, when an opportunity is afforded to weed out those whose presence might prove dangerous. This examination is not repeated, which is perhaps unfortunate, as a half-yearly test would not be a lengthy operation if conducted on the same lines as the examination of recruits.

An exception is made in favour of those who are employed in departments where metallic paints are handled or where powders are used, as in ink-grinding workshops and in those where minerals are pulverized; men employed in these workshops are examined once a month.

Medical examination having secured for the Works a body of workers all in good health, to ensure their remaining so elaborate precautions are taken. The loftiness of the workshops tends to make them cold, which is counteracted by a system of warming by hot air. It is worth noting that the Plenum system is everywhere in force, as it is the only means of satisfactorily controlling the inflow. Ventilation is therefore perfectly easy, and is regulated by fans varying in power with the requirements of the departments. The all-important problem of ventilation and air space has been completely solved at Port Sunlight, and it is significant that the factory inspectors have never registered even an insignificant complaint against the conditions. This will cause no surprise when we compare them with the legal minimum.

The Factory Act, 1901, enacts as follows:—

"Part I. Section III.—A factory shall for the purposes of this Act, and a workshop shall for the purposes of the law relating to public health be deemed to be so overcrowded as to be dangerous or injurious to the health of the persons employed therein, if the number of cubic feet of space in any room therein bears to the number of persons employed at one time in the room a proportion less than two hundred and fifty, or, during any period of overtime, four hundred cubic feet of space to every person."

It will be realized how fully the Port Sunlight Works satisfy these very moderate provisions when it is known that this minimum is exceeded never by less than fifteen times and in certain parts as much as twenty. This highly important fact is established by the sampling of the air in the workshops, which has been effected from time to time; carbon monoxide, the most dangerous of industrial by-products, does not exist even as a trace; carbon dioxide, the natural product of the human breathing process, a non-toxic but inert gas, does not average more than half the maximum allowed by the Home Office regulations. All this tends to prove that the air is as chemically pure as can be desired and no medical man or enlightened factory owner will deny that this must react very favourably upon the quality of the work, for there is no disputing the fact that air heavily laden with even inert gases tends to dull the faculties of the worker and to stupefy his reasoning powers. Apart, therefore, from humanitarian motives, there is no doubt that the policy pursued at Port Sunlight in this connection has been productive of valuable results.

Minor precautions have, moreover, been taken to ensure the comfort of the workers. In the cardboard-box room, for instance, a good deal of vegetable dust is created; this is not dangerous, but the employees, who are all girls, have been provided with white canvas hoods which enable them to keep their hair clean; a small matter no doubt, but interesting as an evidence of kindly forethought. Provisions of a similar nature, but which do not come strictly within the category of safety measures, are set forth in the next chapter.

TYPICAL SAFETY MEASURES.—Typical safety measures are, however, those which are designed to protect the workers against the influence of dust; it is notorious that even non-poisonous substances, such as coal, stone, metals, etc., have, when in the form of fine dust, the most serious effects upon the respiratory organs, and upon all mucous tissue in general; for instance, miner's phthisis, so common in stone and metal mines, has not yet been completely rooted out by the spray and the respirator. The difficulties with which the Port Sunlight management has to contend are, as regards these particular diseases, comparatively small, for the only workshops in need of protection against them are those in which ink is ground, wood sawn, and mineral powder handled. In all these departments the employees have been supplied with respirators, but it is interesting to note that the men passively resist the introduction. I did not see a single respirator in use; this is a common occurrence, especially in mines, where the floors are often found littered with these preventives after the gangs have come up. This is comprehensible, for hard work is rendered far harder if anything impedes the worker's breathing.

Far more efficacious means than respirators are in use at Port Sunlight. In the wood-box room, for instance, powerful fans draw off the sawdust so completely that one can hardly believe that one is in a carpentry workshop, for one misses the familiar litter of sawdust and shavings; the velocity of the fans is low, so as to avoid draughts, but their volume is very large. Some idea of the amount of work done by them can be gained from a visit to the metal cylinder, nine feet long and seven feet in diameter, which is to be seen just outside the workshop; the exhausts communicate with this cylinder and, in spite of its enormous capacity, often fill it in one or two days with as much sawdust as would cover the floor of the workshop a foot deep if not extracted.

Similar methods are used in the ink-grinding and mineral-powder room, where, owing to the more dangerous influence of the dust, they are needed to a greater degree. There, over every grinding-table or powder-pan, an inverted funnel is fixed, the broad opening not being more than fifteen to eighteen inches from the material. The velocity of the fans is here much greater, the draught being strong enough to draw in a sheet of cardboard; as a result, hardly a speck of powder can be seen floating in the air in a portion of the workshop where some dozen of these implements are at work.

Owing to the fact that machinery is employed in every department, from boiler-room to packing-room, accidents are more likely of occurrence than industrial disease; they have, however, been reduced to a minimum. In the pan room, for instance, not only has every pan been surrounded by a bulwark some three and three-quarters feet high, but, to avoid any danger of an overflow, the introduction of steam into the boiling substance is regulated by three separate injectors, which allows of the shutting off of one-third of the steam or, if required, of two-thirds, or even the whole. The machinery is screened, not only in conformity with, but in excess of, official requirements. Much of it is railed in by wood panelling some four feet high; indeed, there is reason to think that in some cases convenience of handling has been sacrificed to safety, and that a man injured by the machinery must have been negligent. Screening is in fact a feature of the plant, and it is regrettable that similar standards are not yet imposed by law. Apart from these measures, however, steps have been taken to make the machinery fool-proof by the profuse application of posters. These do not only tell the employee how to use the machinery, but they forbid cleaning and oiling whilst it is in motion, and, under certain conditions prohibit the use of it altogether. Special apparatus is provided in some cases; I was able to note a tin-stamping machine to which a simply worded caution is affixed, giving directions as to method of use and instructing the worker to unclog it, in case of need, not with his hands but with a special brass pricker which is chained to the machine. Nevertheless, a female employee was wounded by this machine some months ago owing to her having disregarded instructions and having attempted to regulate it by hand instead of using the pricker; this tends to show that no precautions can cope with stupidity and, therefore, how important it is that the stupid should be protected against themselves. So far has this protection gone that a subway has been built to obviate the necessity of the employees crossing the railway lines.

There exists at Port Sunlight a particularly interesting institution, the Personal Accident Inquiries Committees, the object of which is to reduce misadventure still further. It is clear that every accident reads a lesson; indeed, it is painful to think that almost every improvement in industrial conditions is traceable either to an intolerable state of things or to a serious accident. It is, however, important that the lesson should be learned at a minimum cost of life and suffering, and it is for this purpose that these committees have been created; as they are somewhat unusual, and yet so fertile in possibilities, the rules are here reproduced *in extenso*—

Personal Accident Inquiries.

Rules.

1. With the object of further minimizing the number of preventable accidents in the Factory, the undermentioned Committees will be constituted.

2. The principal duties of each Committee shall be—

(*a*) To promptly and fully inquire into and report to the Company upon any personal accident happening in the division represented by the Committee, which prevents the injured person from following his or her usual occupation for at least three working days after the accident, and the cause of same, and to make recommendations so as, if possible, to prevent the repetition of such accidents. The Committee shall have power to visit the site, make full inspection, hear witnesses, and generally investigate all the circumstances connected with the accident.

(*b*) When specially requested by the Company to do so, to recommend the compensation (if any) to be offered to any injured person or persons. It is not hereby sought to bind such person or persons to accept such compensation.

(*c*) To nominate quarterly two members of the Committee who, along with the Divisional Manager and a Foreman nominated by the Company, shall make periodical inspection of the Division, point out defects (if any), and make recommendations calculated to prevent accidents of any kind.

(*d*) To have proper minutes kept of the proceedings at every inquiry and meeting of the Committee.

3. A meeting of the Committee shall also be convened, whether or not a personal accident has happened, whenever required by the Company, or whenever, in the opinion of at least three members of the Committee, any circumstances have arisen which render a meeting of the Committee desirable.

4. Committees, as follow, will be formed to represent the following divisions of the Factory, respectively, viz.:

SOAPMAKING DEPARTMENTS	Number of Employee Representatives
No. 1 Pan Room	2
No. 2 Pan Room	1
Lyes Rooms (Nos. 1 & 2) ..	1
Cleansers (Nos. 1 & 2) ..	1
	5

SOAP WORKS DEPARTMENTS (Males).	Number of Employee Representatives
Timber Sheds	1
No. 1 Box Room	1
No. 2 Box ,, ...	1
No. 1 Frame ,, ...	2
No. 2 Frame ,, ...	1
No. 1 Stamping Room ..	1
	7

Soap Works Departments (Females).	Number of Employee Representatives
No. 1 Stamping Room	2
No. 2 Stamping Room	2
	4

Chemical Departments.	
Melting Out and Mixing	1
Glycerine Recovery	1
Glycerine Refinery	1
Alkali No. 1	1
Alkali Nos. 2 and 3	1
Cotton Seed Mill	1
	6

No. 3 Soap Works (Males).	
Woodbox Making	1
Toilet Making	2
Dry Soap and Ski Making	1
Monkey Brand and Vim Making	1
	5

No. 3 Soap Works (Females).	
Toilet Packing	1
Lux Packing	2
Monkey Brand, Vim, Ski, and Dry Soap Packing	1
	4

Printing Department (Males).	
Printing—Tradesmen	1
Printing—Labourers	1
Compositors	1
Electro and Stereo	1
Cardbox	1
Tinbox and Printing	1
Paper Warehouse	1
	7

Printing Department. (Females).	Number of Employee Representatives
Folding Cardbox	2
Rigid Cardbox	1
Printing	1
Tinbox	1
Picture Framing	1
	6

Engineering Department.	
Tradesmen	2
Labourers	1
Boilermen and Enginemen	1
Electrical	1
	5

Buildings.	
Tradesmen	2
Labourers	1
Machinists	1
	4

Traffic.	
Wharf	2
Warehouse	1
Yard and Carters	1
	4

Cross River.	
Flat Captains	2
Mates	1
	3

5. Each Committee will consist of the Divisional Manager and the Foreman in the division (being Company nominees) and/or other nominees of the Company, and an equal number of male Employees (being Employee nominees) with not less than two years' continuous service, elected from amongst themselves by the male Employees in the division. Any person with less than three months' continuous service shall not be entitled to vote on such election. The proportion which the number of Employee nominees from one department of a division shall bear to the total number of Employee nominees for that division shall, from time to time, be fixed by the Company. For the purpose of regulating any Committee under this rule, the Company may at any time require one or more members of the Committee to resign his office as such member. The member or members so to resign to be decided by ballot.

6. A Committee shall also be formed for each division in which females are employed, and all the provisions of these Rules shall apply to such Committee, subject to the following variations:—

(*a*) The Committee shall consist of the Divisional Manager and the Forewoman or Overlookers in the Division (being Company nominees) and/or other nominees of the Company and an equal number of female Employees (being Employee nominees) with not less than two years' continuous service, elected from amongst themselves by the female Employees in the Division.

(*b*) Where necessary, words importing the masculine gender shall be read as importing the feminine gender.

7. The Divisional Manager shall act as convener of inquiries and meetings, or, in his absence, such other person as may be nominated by the Company.

8. At least four members of the Committee shall form a quorum for any inquiry or meeting, two of whom must be Company nominees and two Employee nominees.

9. Each inquiry and meeting will be presided over by the Divisional Manager, unless the General Works Manager, or some other person nominated by the Company for such purpose, shall elect to preside.

10. Each member of Committee shall have one vote on every resolution. The Divisional Manager, when presiding, shall have a casting vote.

11. The Committee may require any member (except the Divisional Manager) who, in their opinion, may be directly concerned in or affected by any inquiry or proceedings, to abstain from voting on any resolution thereat.

12. The Company may nominate any person or persons, not being a member or members of the Committee, to be present and take part in the proceedings at any inquiry or meeting, but he or they shall not vote thereat.

13. Inquiries and meetings may be held alternately in the Company's and the members' own time.

14. No member of any Committee shall be entitled to claim any payment or remuneration for any services rendered or work done by him as such member.

15. The Company may, at any time, at its discretion, alter, vary, or annul these rules or disband all or any of the Committees, and its decision as to any matter or question arising as to the construction, interpretation, or spirit of these rules shall be final.

The working of this institution will be understood from the rules, and it is unnecessary to enlarge upon the value of the services which it renders. Two points only need be emphasized; one is the fact that sixty employees are thereby given a direct interest in the internal government of the factory—a very desirable result, which must contribute to increase the social value of both electors and elect; the other is the fact that the administration is thoroughly democratic, as is shown by the stress laid in Rules 5, 6, and 8 on the equality of the voting power of masters and men. It should be added that there has certainly been a considerable decrease in the accident rate; findings are posted in the department in which the casualty took place and all the managers are notified; this adequate publicity has been fully justified by results.

THE AMBULANCE CORPS.—However minute precautions may be, accidents must and do happen; it is therefore interesting to say a few words about the Port Sunlight Ambulance Corps and Surgeries. Every section of the Works is provided with a surgery, where patients are attended to by the ambulance corps until the doctor has arrived. The corps itself consists of twenty men and several women, all of whom are employees; they must hold a St. John's Association certificate, and are re-examined every year. Members wear a badge while on duty, and they are rendered available at all times by means of placards fixed in every department giving their names and stating where they are to be found. These men receive one shilling per week over and above their wages and one shilling per drill, which takes place monthly. They are under the general control of the Village medical officer and, while at their ordinary work, of the Works manager. It should be added that, in the Village itself, there is a branch of the St. John's Association, of which most of the Works ambulance corps are members; it numbers altogether about forty men, most of whom are available in the Works when required.

FIRE PREVENTION.—It only now remains to refer to the precautions that have been taken against fire. They are very minute, which would seem superfluous in view of the fact that the Works are built of brick and steel, but the stores of wood and fats are a source of danger against which provision must be made. It should be said that, even should an outbreak of fire take place, it appears impossible that lives could be lost, thanks to the numerous exits. The buildings are certainly well protected in the first instance: where there are two storeys fireproof floors have been fitted; double doors, also fireproof, separate the departments; the Works are surrounded and intersected by fresh water mains. So far there is every reasonable security, but more ample provision against fire has been made. Every department is provided with automatic fire alarms and with automatic sprinklers in the roof at every ten feet. These sprinklers are fed by tanks containing four to five hundred thousand gallons, over and above the supply from the mains; all the valves are tested once a week by the fire superintendent. In addition, all departments are provided with chemical extinguishers and hand pumps, and rows of sand buckets can be seen in readiness near the fat stores. As regards the closed timber stores, it is interesting to note that these are so arranged as to allow of each being hermetically sealed in the event of a conflagration; thus the fire would in a few minutes be stifled for want of air. The fire brigade consists of six men, including the superintendent, who are permanently employed in this capacity and receive an additional shilling per weekly drill; sixteen men are drawn from the Works and are trained on the same lines and receive the same pay, so that the brigade numbers twenty-two men. A valuable innovation has been the introduction of a bonus system, producing about two shillings per week for each man, which is payable in the event of there having been no greater loss by fire during each half-year than altogether £50. As a result the brigade is exceedingly watchful, and many incipient fires, instead of remaining unobserved for a few precious minutes, are dealt with at once. So efficacious has this system been that, during the last six years, no bonus has been lost, *i.e.* six years' work has resulted in less than £300 damages by fire—a notable record.

It will be seen from the above that every conceivable device has been resorted to to ensure the safety of both workers and Works. I would repeat that it is not within the scope of this book to study the Works themselves and the processes of manufacture, but this somewhat lengthy analysis of safety measures, in so far as they affect the social aspects of the Village, is undoubtedly essential. From the point of view of working conditions, an important chapter is the next, where the internal *régime* of the Factory is passed under review, and also the position of the employees as regards nature and hours of labour, remuneration, and personal treatment.

CHAPTER III

THE WORKS: RÉGIME OF THE WORKERS

IMPROVED safety appliances and modern hygienic methods naturally make for an improvement in the quality of work done, as well as in the health and spirits of the workers, but, beyond this, it is of importance that these should enter into good relations with their employers, and so, in business as in other fields, be enabled to realize their manhood. A fair, if firm, rule forms a sound basis for this good understanding; it is well that a man should have to give of his best while at work, provided that he be justly treated, that his hours be not over long, and that he find within easy reach opportunities for relaxation and amusement.

A visit to the Port Sunlight Works certainly shows that no time is wasted; the casual observer cannot conceive of greater activity or expedition, but relations between the workers and their foremen appear to be good, and there is in most of the workshops an atmosphere of good temper and good-will. There is no loitering, partly, no doubt, owing to the military precision of the Factory, partly owing to the zest with which the employees go to work. Rules are evidently not allowed to fall into abeyance; for instance, tobacco chewing is forbidden; if, after a warning, the offence is repeated the offender is dismissed. As a result the floors are everywhere clean and the general hygiene of the Factory is much improved. This will serve to show that even trifles are not overlooked. The firmness of the rule is, however, coupled with the effort that is made to develop the individuality of the men, as exemplified by the Accident Committee (Chapter II.).

THE SUGGESTION BOX.—Another interesting example is the Suggestion Box, placed in every department. The object of this institution is, on the one hand, to reap for the Works the benefit of the men's powers of observation and invention, on the other to interest them in their work and thus to develop their brains. Any employee who sees a way of improving the output, simplifying some process, minimizing the possibility of accidents, or by some means improving working conditions, can make out his suggestion on a desk specially provided in his department and deposit it in the Suggestion Box. The keys are in the hands of the Suggestion Bureau; each division of the Works has its committee, which includes foremen and the divisional manager. These committees delegate each its chairman to the Suggestion Council, which is presided over by the general manager. The boxes are opened periodically, when the suggestions are dealt with by the committee whose work they affect; this committee has power to reject them or, if they appear valuable, to send them up to the council for further consideration. Should the council consider them worth taking up they are sent to the Management. Important suggestions go to the Board. The best of these ideas are rewarded with prizes, varying in value between 5*s.* and £20; adopted suggestions are always paid for, and if it were worth while to patent any one of them the employee would receive the royalties. The results of the system have been excellent; suggestions are every year made by the hundred, and a certain number are useful. Apart from the training thus given to the workers, in certain cases important results have followed. I was shown, for instance, a machine where the operator was formerly very liable to have her finger tips caught; indeed accidents often happened: as a result of an employee's suggestion a movable top was introduced, an exceedingly ingenious contrivance which lifts the operator's hand out of danger and makes an accident impossible. For this device the employee received a substantial cash prize and a patent was taken out in his name; he now receives a royalty on every such appliance fixed in other factories.*

Good feeling is also kept up in other minor ways. I referred in Chapter II. to the hoods that are supplied to the girls in certain departments; in every workshop the girls are supplied with overalls free of charge; these are washed once a week. Some of the men, if engaged in particularly dirty work, are likewise provided for in this way. Complaints of any description may be addressed direct to the Works manager or to the chairman of the Company, without the intervention of the foremen; this contributes to keep up confidence and good feeling. If

* Messrs. Lever Brothers pay no royalty, but, in addition to the cash prize, defray the cost of patenting.

overtime has to be worked the men are allowed half an hour's break, and the girls (during this break) who cannot legally work beyond seven o'clock are given a free tea. In these and many other ways much is done to ensure good feeling, over and above the institutions to which reference is made further on.

HOURS AND WAGES.—As regards hours and wages, conditions at Port Sunlight compare well with those that prevail in most factories. The day begins for men at 7.50 A.M. and ends at 5.30 P.M., one hour being allowed for dinner; girls are employed from 8 to 5, also with one hour's allowance at midday; on Fridays all leave at 5.30, and on Saturdays at 12.30. Thus the girls are secured a 45-hour week and the men exactly a 48-hour week, or eight hours a day. Compared with the usual conditions of labour these are excellent, and there is a consensus of opinion among the managers that the work has benefited as much as the worker; the day is not too long, but it is well filled, and there is none of the slackness in the later hours that characterizes factories where the men are employed for nine or ten hours. It is good to think that an arrangement can benefit both employer and employee, a state of affairs which is all too rare. Incidentally it is worth noting that the men enter the Works ten minutes before the girls, and leave them half an hour later; the object of this arrangement is not so much to enable the men to put in three hours per week more work than the girls, for this might have been achieved otherwise, as to arrange for the girls to be away from the scene when the Works open and close for the men. It would not be conducive to discipline for the 2000 men and boys and the 1600 girls to leave the Works in a confused stream, particularly during the reaction following upon release from work. For this purpose ten minutes have been found sufficient in the morning, for the girls rarely anticipate the time of opening, while in the evening half an hour is fully necessary to clear them from Port Sunlight.

The bulk of the labour employed at Port Sunlight is unskilled; the number of casuals varies all the year round between 200 and 250. Trade Union rates are paid in all cases, and it is worth noting that, where the Union rules allow of a working week exceeding 48 hours, at Port Sunlight the full rate is paid for the short week. This has resulted in good relations with the Unions, so good that there has never been a strike at the Works, nor has there been even a threat of one. The girls are paid 5*s.* to 10*s.* a week as learners, and can earn 12*s.* to 15*s.* a week on piece work; boys (under 21) 5*s.* to 22*s.* a week; the men (all over 21) receive a minimum wage of 22*s.* a week, but most of them are paid about 25*s.* It is interesting to note that up to some time ago the minimum wage was the average of the district, *i.e.* 20*s.* a week; it was increased without any demand from the men, because the management held that 20*s.* was too low a level for a family. The minimum wage is paid to all the male workers over 21, even to those who are engaged on piece work. These receive 22*s.* a week and any excess they may have earned; should they have earned less than 22*s.* they still receive that sum, and the difference is debited against them and repaid later when they once more exceed the minimum. The Works are liable to lose by this system if a man dies or leaves, for in the latter case no claim is made against him, but the object of the system is actually to secure the minimum wage for all. These wages have never created discontent, partly, no doubt, owing to the advantages conferred on those who live in the Village and to the various conveniences described further on, which are at the disposal of employees of both sexes. Before passing on to other questions, it should be observed that under no circumstances are children under fourteen employed at the Works, and that the same rule applies to married women. As soon as a girl marries she is looked upon as a "housekeeper" and debarred from employment in the Works, exceptions being occasionally made for widows and for a few special cases. It is hardly necessary to emphasize the importance of this rule; the evils that follow in the train of industrial work for married women—work which to the shame of England is sometimes persisted in up to the day when the woman gives birth to a child—are so notorious that it is needless to enlarge upon them, any more than upon the results of such work on the home, upon the health and the education of growing children. To close the subject of hours and pay, it should be said that clerks work from 8.30 to 5, and on Saturdays from 8.30 to 12.30; in common with the workmen they are paid time and a-half for overtime. A peculiar feature of this overtime system is that instead of being paid out at the end of the week earnings are credited to the employee; a portion of the accumulation may be withdrawn at Christmas or left for the annual holiday. Should a man be off duty on account of illness or for any other reason, late at his work, etc., he receives his usual wages and deductions are made against his overtime account.

WHAT IS DONE FOR GIRLS.—Far more is done in the Factory for the girls than for the men; but this is explained by the fact that they are mostly very young and can only earn small wages. Cloak rooms are provided for both sexes; they are ventilated and warmed, every employee having a numbered peg. Attached is a drying-room, an important adjunct, for it enables the girls to hang up their wet clothes in an atmosphere heated to about 100 degrees, boots being placed on a special grating; after two or three hours clothing is absolutely dry. This system probably saves the Port Sunlight girls many a chill. The forewomen have a special room.

Each division of the Works is provided with a rest room for the girls; this is an apartment to which any girl who feels unwell may retire for some time on applying to the forewoman; it is destined for slight and temporary indispositions only, and furnished plainly but prettily with cane chairs and sofas. Though the walls are lined with coloured tiles and hung with pictures, and the floor is covered with green linoleum, I am afraid these rooms are too severely hygienic to be really comfortable; there never was a cosy room that was not stuffy as well. However, it is not intended to make the rest room a club; a matron is in attendance, but it is said that her services are not often required. Attached is a surgery, fitted mainly for accidents, where employees can always be treated gratis.

The girls also benefit, on application to the fore-woman, by the shower baths, both hot and cold, which are provided free of charge. The girls are brought up in batches in the firm's time (I could not ascertain whether this was intended to promote cleanliness by placing before the girls the alternative of "work or wash"), and are provided with soap, towels, and rubber caps. Considerable use is made of this privilege. Washing facilities are given in every department in the shape of troughs, soap, and towels; it is regrettable that the water should not be warm, so as to make washing easy and, especially, not to discourage the workers from washing in the winter; this could easily be done by using exhaust steam as a means of heating the water.

WORKERS' RESTAURANTS.—Facilities outside the Factory are so numerous that it becomes essential to distinguish closely between institutions connected with the Works and institutions connected with the workers. Strictly speaking, the Village institutions, which are open to all the employees, should come under the second heading, but it is better to study separately those which are connected solely with the work at the Factory; they are four in number: Gladstone Hall, Hulme Hall, the Holiday Club, and the Old Age Pension scheme.

Gladstone Hall and Hulme Hall are both workers' restaurants, the former being reserved for the men and the latter for the girls; but they are conducted on different principles and must, therefore, be described separately. Both institutions are practically necessary, for New Ferry and Bebington are both about half a mile from the Works and, at any rate, could not accommodate a tenth of the employees during the dinner hour. Gladstone Hall

GLADSTONE HALL.

[*To face p.* 46.

is practically opposite the Works; it is a large hall about seventy-five feet by fifty (seating space alone), with a high vaulted roof and enormous windows and top-lights. As it can and does seat eight hundred diners at a time, it is not superfluous to say that ventilation is secured by three large doors and by fifteen ventilators in the roof over and above the windows. Gladstone Hall is beautifully designed, the vault being broken only by three fifty-foot cross-beams, and the windows being of the usual casement type favoured at Port Sunlight; its walls are profusely decorated with oil paintings. At one end is a stage with footlights and flies complete, the other end being occupied by a stand for the cinematograph; thus it is easy to make use of the hall for other purposes than those of the restaurant. It has been used for political meetings, dances, etc., and is fully licensed for stage plays, music, and dancing; a clever arrangement is that of the tables, which can drop into halves and be turned in a short time into seats with backs. The hall is warmed by steam and lighted by electricity. Its outer aspect is pleasant, for it is built in the "English cottage" style, of which so many examples have been erected at Garden City; moreover, it stands in its own grounds and is covered with creepers. The interest of Gladstone Hall lies, however, not so much in the facilities it affords for entertainment as in its daily use as a restaurant for the men. Those who live in the Village go home, but so many live out that the eight hundred seats are none too many; moreover, it is not a preserve of the Company's employees, and it is used by such men as carters, etc., whose work detains them at Port Sunlight during the dinner hour. The staff will cook any food that the men may bring before going to work or warm such dishes as pies or stews. For these purposes a large oven is provided, the warming of the meals being done by steam, so that burning becomes impossible; this, as also the supply of utensils, cans, hot water, and salt is free, the cans and hot water being required for the making of coffee and tea which the men bring with them. Gladstone Hall is also available free of cost for the men who bring cold dishes. Of course no intoxicants are allowed, nor is any food or drink sold; Gladstone Hall does not undertake to provide dinners. I could not help thinking it desirable that it should do so, particularly in view of the success of Hulme Hall, described further on; it is certainly a boon for the workers to have their dinners kept warm and a comfortable hall provided, but it would be still better to run a restaurant on a self-supporting basis as is done at Hulme Hall. However, the hall is extensively patronized and proceedings are remarkably orderly; the caterer and his assistants have no difficulty in keeping down horseplay, spitting, etc.; several large tubs are provided for refuse, so that it is easy to keep the hall clean by swabbing the floor daily and scrubbing it once a week with deck brushes.

In connection with Gladstone Hall are two dinner clubs, run respectively by the male and female clerks. Each of these clubs has a special room and governs itself by its own committee; both pay a nominal rent, and engage their own cook and staff; they also elect a caterer from among themselves. Messrs. Lever Brothers merely supply utensils, crockery, and coal, which entails hardly any extra expense, for the Hall

GLADSTONE HALL.

[*To face p.* 48.

range is used, and the members of both clubs take it in turn to do their own waiting. These clubs are very successful and supply five dinners a week, for which the men pay 3*s.* and the girls 2*s.* 6*d.* The meal comprises soup, meat, two vegetables, and a sweet. The men's club numbers about 70 members, and the girls' 20. Most of the girls go to Hulme Hall, which is as suitable for the clerks as for the Factory girls, as will be gathered from the following description.

Interesting as Gladstone Hall may be, it fades into insignificance by the side of Hulme Hall, the girls' restaurant. This is an enormous building, standing in a garden about a minute's walk from the Works; its size will be realized not only from its measurements (length 170 feet, breadth 48 to 90 feet) but from the fact that it can accommodate simultaneously 1800 diners. It is of the high vaulted type favoured at Port Sunlight, and is flooded with light by means of its glazed roof; the walls are tiled and covered with pictures, most of them originals of soap advertisements and cleverly drawn. Hulme Hall was opened in 1901, and cost about £18,000 to build; it is an exceedingly successful venture. Every day it provides about 1500 dinners with ease and expedition; there are six counters where tea, soup, dinners, puddings, and cakes are sold, the sixth being reserved for the free distribution of hot water and utensils. The speed with which serving is carried out is remarkable, for there are no attendants: the girls file up to the counters in order; there is no pushing and no quarrelling, so much so that there is no need for a superintendent, and that it is possible to converse in ordinary tones in the midst of 1500 girls having dinner; speed of service is facilitated by checks purchased at the Works. This obviates the necessity for taking money in the Hall. Hulme Hall is open to all the female employees, even to those who choose to bring their own provisions; these, as well as those electing to buy their dinner at the Hall, are provided, free of charge, with utensils (enamel mug, coffee or tea pot, tray, and spoon) and hot water. Most of the girls, however, prefer to make use of the Hulme Hall menu; the reason for this will be realized from the following bill of fare, which does not vary very much:—

Dinner (meat, potatoes, vegetables) ..	2*d.*
Steak Pie	2*d.*
Milk Pudding	1*d.*
Boiled „	1*d.*
Soup and Bread	1*d.*
Tea	½*d.*
Tart	1*d.*
Bread and Butter (4 slices)	1*d.*
Sandwiches	1*d.*

For 3*d.* or 4*d.* it is therefore possible for a girl to obtain a hot dinner; I inspected the portions and they did not appear illiberal; at any rate an extra 1*d.*, making a total of 5*d.*, brings the standard up to a level adequate for a young girl employed on sedentary work. In view of these prices it is amazing that Hulme Hall is self-supporting; it is run entirely by Messrs. Lever Brothers, and is therefore hardly a Village institution; of course it does not realize profits, but it defrays the cost of food, cooking, light,

HULME HALL.

[*To face p.* 50.

and attendance. This should not be lost sight of, for it is not desirable to give a bonus of this kind to the workers, and it is obviously better for them that they should pay the full value of their food, benefiting only by co-operation.

A HOLIDAY CLUB.—A more unusual feature than either of these restaurants is the holiday club. The importance of a holiday for the worker is often not sufficiently recognized; it is difficult to understand why the employer considers his manager, traveller, or clerk is in need of rest for at least one or two weeks a year, and how it is that he does not realize the equally great need of the manual labourer; it is probably another case of defective visualization, to which, as much as to hardness of heart, we can trace much of the misery that afflicts our working population. At Port Sunlight, however, the necessity for holidays has been understood. Every employee who has worked in the Factory since October 1, is eligible for a week's holiday the following summer at full pay, provided he has joined the holiday club. This institution is open to all the employees, and has been established for the purpose of making the holiday a success, by interesting the worker in the formation of a small special fund; the management is entirely in the hands of a committee elected by the male and female employees. The holiday week's full pay that the worker receives is taken as mortgaged by the needs of the family; the special cost of the holiday is defrayed by the weekly deduction of one hour's pay from the employee's wages. On the value of these 51 hours, the Company allows 4 per cent. per completed 4*s*., the total being paid out when the employee decides to take his holiday; the system is therefore, roughly, one of half-shares, the employee supplying 51 hours' pay, and the Company 48 hours, plus interest on deductions. For the clerks a different arrangement prevails; they receive 15 days' holiday at full pay, plus their overtime, as has already been explained; they are not eligible to the holiday club. It is worth noticing among the rules that (1) females and boys rated at under 12*s.* a week contribute 3*d.* per week, (2) any person may, on resigning membership, withdraw his total contributions without interest, an important point in view of the fluctuating nature of the employment. The holiday club is the most successful institution in the Village; in 1907 almost every eligible person had joined, and holidays had been taken by 1098 men and 745 women and girls. It is good to know that the value of play has been realized both by employers and employees, and there is no reason to think that the institution will in the future do anything but flourish.

A PENSION FUND.—We now come to the most important of the four Works' institutions, namely, Old Age Pensions. Long service in general is fully recognized at Port Sunlight, where every employee who has completed 15 years' service receives a gold watch, a certificate, and a silver badge. More solid benefits than these are, however, essential if we are to avoid the tragedy of the aged workman ruthlessly scrapped like worn-out machinery, if we are to save him from the stigma which is attached by an ungrateful country to the receipt of poor relief. It should by this time be acknowledged that old age pensions are a right and not a dole, and that a man earns it as

HULME HALL KITCHEN.

[*To face p.* 52.

fully in a workshop as in a government office; however, I need not dilate upon the subject, for old age pensions are practically accepted by all parties, and are slowly, too slowly, materializing. Meanwhile, something has been done by several important firms and the system in vogue at Port Sunlight is worthy of our consideration.

The "Employees' Benefit Fund" was started in 1904. Its objects are threefold: to grant a retiring pension to every worker after a given period of service, to provide for those who are compelled to retire owing to ill-health or injury, and to pension off the widows of employees. Before dealing with the conditions under which these allowances are granted it is necessary to obtain an idea of the basis and working of the fund. The monies are provided in their entirety by the Company, and no deduction is made from wages; the sole fact of being an employee of Messrs. Lever Brothers is a sufficient qualification; the pension is therefore of the "general and non-contributory" type, which is alone accepted nowadays by the more advanced school of reformers as entirely satisfactory. In the Trust Deed there is no precise statement of the amounts that the Company shall pay in; the contribution is voluntary and may be stopped, the Company making itself liable for no more than "a sum sufficient to place the fund on a sound financial basis." This, in the case of a small firm, would be a weak point, but it is hardly worth considering in the present case, and, at any rate, since the employees invest nothing they run no risk. On the other hand, the Company cannot withdraw any sum once paid in, and interest and dividends go to swell the capital of the fund. In 1907 the sum of £8000 was paid in.

The management of the fund is vested in eight trustees, four of whom represent the Company and four the employees; the employer-trustees are chosen from among the directors, general manager, and secretary; the employee-trustees must be workmen or clerks: managers, heads of departments, and foremen are ineligible. In these elections (which take place every three years) every employee, male and female, has one vote per trustee seat. Since an employee-trustee, on promotion, for instance to foremanship, must resign his post, there is no doubt that representation is democratic; the Trust Deed provides, moreover, that, under any circumstances employer and employee representatives must be equal in number, with the sole reservation that an employer-trustee must preside, and that he has a casting vote.

The benefits under the fund have already been stated. The old age pension is granted to every male aged 65 who has completed 20 years' service, and to every female aged 60 who has been employed for the same period; it amounts to one-eightieth of the last year's salary or wages multiplied by the number of years of service, but cannot exceed £180 a year.

Example A.

An employee receiving salary or wages amounting to 38*s.* 6*d.* a week, or say, £100 per annum, retires (if a male at age 65, and if a female at age 60) after 40 years' service. The trustees would pay

HULME HALL: A COUNTER.

[*To face p.* 54.

him or her an allowance amounting to one-eightieth part of £100 multiplied by 40, or £50 per annum.

Should the employee retire after 20 years' service, but before the age of 65 and 60 respectively (provided that ill-health or injury be not caused by the employee's culpable negligence or misconduct) the trustees are empowered to pay out a similar allowance.

Example B.

An employee receiving a salary or wages amounting to 38*s.* 6*d.* a week, or say, £100 per annum, retires at age (say 45) after 20 years' service, owing to ill-health or accidental injury. The trustees have power to pay one-eightieth of £100 multiplied by 20, or £25 per annum.

This does not interfere with the benefit conferred by the Workmen's Compensation Acts; the trustees are in these cases guided solely by circumstances, and make or do not make an allowance as they may think fit.

Should a male employee who has qualified by 20 years' service die before he has reached the age of 65 (or die while in receipt of a pension), the trustees may grant the widow one-half of that to which the man would have been entitled had he retired at the time of his death, and, in addition, one-fifth of the allowance for every child, the total not to exceed £90 per annum. In the first case, quoted above, had the pensioner died leaving a widow and four children, the widow's allowance would have been £45; this would have been paid to her during her widowhood only, and a deduction of £5 would have been made as each child reached the age of 15. The widow of the employee in Example No. 2, who had retired owing to ill-health or injury, would be treated in exactly the same manner. The trustees have power to commute all these allowances for cash payments, but it is very rare that resort is had to this system; the only case in which this is likely to happen is where the pensioner or his widow enters into another employment or business, when the trustees must be consulted under pain of forfeiture of the allowance. Imprudence is guarded against by protecting the pension from creditors; as it is a compassionate allowance, and there is no legal right to it, it cannot be charged in case of debt or assigned by the beneficiary.

This old age pension scheme appears very complete, and is satisfactory in that it places the worker and his family beyond the reach of absolute poverty in his old age, while it does not yield him enough to keep on the same footing as during his last year of employment. For instance, in Example No. 1, we find that an employee in receipt of 38*s*. 6*d*. a week is granted a pension of £50, or about 19*s*. 3*d*. a week; he is placed on half pay. Knowing this, he will have had every inducement during his working life to save enough to increase his retiring allowance, an inducement which he would not have had if no old age pension had been forthcoming. In Example No. 1, a man who has worked for 40 years, and whose wages are at the end of this period 38*s*. 6*d*., is hardly likely

HULME HALL: WORKERS AT DINNER.

[*To face p.* 56.

to have saved, under the most favourable circumstances, much more than £300. This at 4 per cent., a reasonably high rate, would yield him £12 per annum or less than 5*s.* a week. This beggarly income would obviously hardly be worth striving for, but it assumes a very different aspect if it is to be an addition to a pension of, say, 19*s.* 3*d.*; it makes all the difference between poverty and comfort, given that pensioners' expenses are reduced at Port Sunlight by the offer to them of smaller cottages, and, in fact, it justifies the idea itself; a pension, so long as it does not become quite equal to the worker's income, is a premium on thrift, because without it thrift is thrown away. The Port Sunlight Works are young, and have as yet but few pensioners, no more than 300 employees having completed 15 years' service. The pensioners occupy at present some of the early small houses, rented at 3*s.* 9*d.* a week, including rates; they are apparently living out a cheerful old age. Provocative of bitter thoughts is the contrast when we consider the unjustifiable misery that drives our respectable poor into the workhouses of our great cities.

ATTITUDE OF THE WORKERS.—Statistics will be given in subsequent chapters to show that the pension list is ultimately likely to be a heavy one, owing to the healthiness of the community; it is quite clear that the combination of good housing and a sanitary factory must tend to this result. It will, however, be more convenient and appropriate to consider such consequences as these further on, because it is impossible to apportion the amounts of beneficial influence due respectively to the Village and the Works. On the other hand, it is interesting to know what the employees themselves think of the conditions under which they labour; they are not uncommunicative in this respect and, personally speaking, I found them ready to talk and generally ready to praise: the grumbler is not unknown in Port Sunlight, but there would be grumblers in Utopia, a standard which the Village does not quite attain as yet. Generally speaking, however, the outlook of the men is cheerful and optimistic, a result which is probably due to their apparently excellent state of health. Some complain of the rates of wages, a question into which I need not enter, but which is sufficiently answered by the fact that in all cases full trade union rates or more are paid.

The true index to the opinion of the workers is the length of their stay at the Factory. When we remember that Port Sunlight is close to two great employing centres, Liverpool and Birkenhead, and that unemployment is no more prevalent in the district than in other industrial centres, the changes among the *personnel* are a fair test of satisfaction. It is rare that a regularly employed worker leaves Port Sunlight of his own free will, though a number of the men are unskilled and naturally of a roving disposition; the numbers of the staff do not, as a rule, vary much more than 10 per cent., this variation being accounted for by some hundreds of casuals, most of whom are girls living with their families. Security of tenure is therefore more assured to the Port Sunlight worker than it usually is in England, and this alone is a considerable factor when we come to consider his happiness and mental development. Few of the men allow themselves to be dismissed without protesting and asking for an interview with the General Manager or the Chairman

HULME HALL KITCHEN. [*To face p.* 58.

of the Company; I understand that this privilege is generally granted, but the fact is interesting as showing how keen the men are to retain their work at Port Sunlight.

Though the firm is young, a number of employees (as before stated) have already completed fifteen years' service; their numbers will obviously increase at a speedier rate as time goes on, since every year that elapses brings into count a larger number of employees, a number roughly proportionate to the development of the business. Within a few years several hundreds of employees will have qualified for the long-service watch and certificate. In many cases the father of the family is employed with his sons and daughters; the inhabitants of the Village are, as a rule, anxious to place their children in the Works, and it is worth noticing that the sons of the villagers have the preference as regards apprenticeships in the skilled trades.

Before dismissing this subject it should be noted that casuals are treated in the same way as men permanently employed. They have the use of the various restaurants and facilities, and may join any of the clubs; when they leave their employment they retain membership of these up to the end of the financial year, or may remain members indefinitely of those clubs which admit outsiders.

The general impressions of the visitor to the Port Sunlight Works can be summed up in three words: "Safety, Health and Order." The most striking of the three is probably the first, for nothing that can possibly be imagined to make machinery and processes fool-proof seems to have been overlooked; of that enough has been said to make it unnecessary to return to the subject. What the health of the community ought to be will be gathered from the illustrations, for they show to what extent light and air are provided for. Order is also impressive, for some departments would seem over-organized, so remarkable is the forethought that has been applied with regard to them. So far as a factory can be a place of pleasure, I do not hesitate to say that, under the present faulty conditions of industrial production, Port Sunlight provides an example which every enlightened manufacturer should make it his object to emulate.

CHAPTER IV

THE VILLAGE: TOPOGRAPHY AND ARCHITECTURE

WHEN we wish to describe a foreign town and to compare it with one of our own cities, it is not as a rule difficult to find means of expressing ourselves. We say that the town suggests Bermondsey or Streatham and are at once understood, but if we try to apply the same rule to Port Sunlight we find an insuperable difficulty before us, because the little township is at the same time a city and a village, because it possesses to an equal degree the cheerfulness of Edgbaston, the formality of Chiswick, and the charming irregularity of Dulwich. Dulwich is perhaps the nearest æsthetic equivalent of Port Sunlight, that is, old Dulwich, not the newer parts, which the builder is steadily disfiguring by means of the "row" system; the houses are smaller and built in blocks instead of standing proudly in their own grounds, but the general impression of greenness and repose is somewhat similar in this Dulwich *in petto.*

The impression of country is strongest when one walks through the Village; from one's window one realizes that it is pretty, but once out in the road one is immediately struck by something unusual, for the footpaths are not entirely paved as one might expect in a town of 3500 souls, but are made of beaten earth like those that are found along some of our high roads, while the middle of the path is paved with flagstones. This trifling circumstance, together with the many trees, both old and newly planted, which often intrude upon the footway, produces a singularly vivid impression of rusticity. Apart, however, from the roads themselves, nothing seems to have been neglected which may produce in the town-dweller the illusion that he has indeed gone back to the land. All the houses are set back from the road, often as much as ten yards, and sometimes more, so that they are protected from the dust and the glare by a broad fringe of small gardens, grass grown and gay with flowers.

GARDEN MANAGEMENT.—The Port Sunlight gardens deserve a chapter to themselves, so numerous and so trim are they. As I have said above, every house is fronted by a garden, which is not attached to it but is kept up by the estate. At one time these front gardens were given up to the tenants, but their æsthetic possibilities were not appreciated; they were used as fowl-runs, and even as dustbins, while the family washing was unblushingly exposed on the palings. The exterior aspect of the Village was being ruined, and the estate office had finally to take these gardens over, and it has been found that central management was more suitable: the results speak for themselves. The gardens are usually about a hundred feet long by about twenty-five to thirty feet broad, and always contain trim lawns, broken here and there by flower beds, trees, and groups of trained shrubs; there, as Mr. E. V. Lucas says of Kensington Gardens, one sees the spring come in as surely and sweetly as in

COTTAGES. [*To face p.* 62.

any Devonshire lane. Behind the gardens appear the little houses, clothed in trailing creepers which overrun windows and porches and rebelliously evade the gardener's hand. I confess to remembering with some sentimental tenderness the glimpses through the creepers that embowered my Bath Street window, of the spreading lawn where a formal little white stone monument retained for a moment the pale rays of the northern sun.

VARIETY OF BUILDINGS.—Singularly attractive, too, is the architecture of the Village, where, perched upon every slope, houses of all styles and colours smile in harmonious array. They are not all beautiful, but all are quaint and fresh, unexpected and engrossing to eyes wearied by the awful monotony of villadom and the pretentiousness of stucco. I shall have something to say further on of these architectural styles, not all of which are quite successful or appropriate, but every one of which bespeaks interest and courageous experiment. It is enough to say that the visitor is at first bewildered by their diversity, and that he realizes to the full the charm of irregularity; the houses are set down in groups of two and three, of five or six, some high, some low, some plain and some ambitious; there is no monotony, and every street has its character, its local nationality.

Irregularity of building does not mean absence of plan, and there is much method in the apparently casual arrangement of the Port Sunlight roads. Though some houses are set back and their roofs are not severely brought into line, the design is calculated only to break through uniformity, not to deflect the straights and the curves of the roads. Port Sunlight has been "town-planned" with great care, and so successfully that this does not appear from a cursory glance, and, to realize it, it is necessary to examine the plan itself. It will be gathered from the description given in Chapter I. of the topography of the Village, that it would have been quite impossible to lay it out on geometrical lines as has been done at Garden City, on account of the deep depressions that once were marshes; had the planning been carried out rigidly most of the main roads would have suffered from gradients of one in ten or been carried over costly bridges. Roughly speaking, Port Sunlight is bounded on the east and on the west by two parallel roads; between these lies a third road which traverses the estate. These three thoroughfares are connected by three principal cross-roads, two of which are practically straight. It will be seen from the appended plan that, as regards the main roads, everything that could be done to preserve regularity has been done, and that, where the dells made regularity impossible, the streets have been laid out so as to follow the undulations of the land. The southern portion of the estate is more fully developed than the northern, and is regular in design; it is likely that the laying out of the newer half will proceed on similar lines; such defects as may be found in the plan are due almost entirely to the lie of the land.

TOWN PLANNING.—The planning of the houses themselves has been most carefully thought out, and it is interesting to analyze this part of the scheme because it is here that the Garden City idea most strongly appears. The building area of Port Sunlight has been divided into small sections each comprising

COTTAGES.

COTTAGES. [To face p. 64.

anything between fifty and one hundred cottages and entirely self-contained; these sections are irregular in shape, but are almost invariably rough quadrilaterals, along each side of which runs a road. The cottages are built so as to face the roads, the back-yards all being turned towards a central area laid out as allotment gardens; in most cases these gardens occupy not less than one-half of the sectional area, an important point as far as sanitary conditions are concerned. By this means the average number of houses per acre is kept at about five, or less than half the ultimate average of Letchworth, the prototype of garden cities. At this stage of social discussions it is unnecessary to lay stress on the importance of this question, but we must remember that however carefully administered, however sanitary a village may be, it cannot be said to have satisfactorily solved the housing problem unless overcrowding be kept down. I mean by this the overcrowding of areas, which is almost as dangerous as the overcrowding of houses. It is possible that, in course of time, the low average of houses per acre which is established at Port Sunlight may be slightly increased to, say, a maximum of eight houses per acre, but the peril is a remote one, if indeed a peril it be to attain a standard well below that accepted at Garden City.

The cottages themselves are not detached, for this has been thought unnecessary; they are not built in "rows," which is a system against which one cannot protest too strongly, but in small groups varying between two and ten; the commonest arrangement consists of seven houses. If we take seven houses as the average number per block, and seventy-five as the average number of houses per section, we find that each section comprises ten to eleven blocks; that is neither too much nor too little, for it allows of ten to eleven variations in style being applied in the same section without inviting too great contrasts which would be destructive of harmony. Generally speaking all the blocks comprised within a section are different, sometimes very different, in style but unified to a certain extent by the use of similar materials. Thus we may find in the same section specimens of Early English and Renaissance architecture, but most of the houses are built of brick and roughcast or with plaster and beams, so that a sufficient degree of uniformity is secured. It would not be desirable to exaggerate differences of style; to turn Port Sunlight into a congeries of architectural experiments would be destructive of the repose that makes it in some ways so much more English than many a secluded hamlet. As it is, all the blocks are not successful, a few being far too ambitious in design, but they are mostly restrained in their lines and rarely offend the eye which they so often please. It is intended, however, to make some more experiments, and the estate office has planned blocks in the French, Belgian, Dutch, German and Italian styles. This idea has not yet been carried out except in the case of a small block which is Belgian in style; the others will probably be erected later on, and will then form a "street of nations."

While the most usual design is Early English, we find it rather difficult to class the architectural styles at Port Sunlight save with reference to materials, for there are not very great variations in design, and the

COTTAGES.

COTTAGES. [*To face p.* 66.

estate relies for its effects mainly on combinations. The materials used in the Village are seven in number: brick (Ruabon), roughcast (grey, white, or yellow), tile, slate, beams (brown or green), plaster (white), and sandstone (red). This affords scope for very varied combinations, many of which are very pleasing to the eye; they fall naturally into groups, and a few words about each of these are not unnecessary.

1. SINGLE-MATERIAL HOUSES.—There are a large number of these if we take "single" material as referring to the walls only, for the roof invariably differs; the "all-brick" house is fortunately but little favoured, for it is a failure, however superior it may be to the box with five holes in which we usually house our working population. These brick houses would appear pretty in Ancoats, for they are graceful enough in design, and relieved as a rule by pointed tiled roofs; but in Port Sunlight they suffer by comparison with more elegant types. The other houses of this group are mainly roughcast; this material lends itself to the more fanciful work than does brick, and most of the cottages shown in the illustrations with white walls are built in this manner. Yellow and grey roughcast occur occasionally, though they are more often used in the second group; yellow roughcast, alone, is rarely seen, for it needs relief: a village built in this material would be a nightmare. Grey roughcast, on the other hand, is very successfully applied at Port Sunlight, and is usually combined with green doors and window-frames, the effect of which is pleasant, though it is eclipsed by the white roughcast. This material is extensively used at Port Sunlight, and anything fresher and more charming than the little

white houses, spotlessly clean, with their French windows, leaded panes, and gaily painted woodwork, I cannot imagine. When this type of house is roofed with pink or crimson tiles, it attains the greatest possible degree of picturesqueness; it is good to see that this has been fully realized, and that the white roughcast cottage is a very frequent type.

2. TWO-MATERIAL HOUSES.—In these dwellings the base is usually brick or sandstone, and the upper part roughcast or plaster. Where the brick base is combined with yellow or grey roughcast the result is unfortunate, for the colours approximate enough to clash, and not enough to harmonize. The combination of a brick or red sandstone base with a white roughcast upper part is, however, very pleasing; some of the prettiest cottages are beyond doubt those in which red sandstone is combined with white roughcast, and tiles in the same tone as the base. In a few cases slate is used as a roof, and contrasts pleasantly with the roughcast; but on the whole its use is discouraged, for it is too dreary under the northern sky.

None of these types are, however, uncommon; we see them more or less successfully carried out in various suburbs and in many cases at Garden City. To Port Sunlight, however, belongs the credit of having built a few cottages of that older type in which England was so rich a hundred years ago, and in which the sunken beam is a feature. It is beyond question that nothing in modern country-house building can compare with this style; at Port Sunlight these cottages are built on a low base of red sandstone, the upper part being made of white plaster into which are sunk broad brown beams. The roofs are pointed,

COTTAGES.

COTTAGES. [*To face p.* 68.

gabled, or fitted with dormer windows, and are built of some dark material, such as wood, slate, or even thatch; thus they preserve the restraint that characterizes this old English style, and, if they were not unfortunately somewhat costly, it would be desirable to increase their numbers very largely. The Post-office, the Library, and the Collegium * are built in this style, and, for that reason alone, rank among the most attractive buildings in the Village.

Apart from materials, the design of the Port Sunlight cottages is worthy of comment. In some cases originality has run rather wild, for most of the blocks have been competed for by architects who had visibly resolved to outshine their competitors; on the whole, however, a measure of simplicity has been preserved. The bay window is a feature, likewise the gable and also the dormer window; here and there we find a turret which we could well spare or a small porch or a verandah which pleases the eye. In a few cases the sloping roofs have been carried too far out and the lines of the rooms have been broken by unexpected recesses and projections, but, generally speaking, space has never been sacrificed to the exigencies of beauty. In one block only (Lower Road) has light been excluded to any extent for the sake of design; there we find a group of seven houses along the front of which runs a verandah supported by pillars which, as it is some four feet broad, effectually excludes sunshine from the ground floor. This is the one and only instance of such a mistake; in all the other cottages the roof is not allowed to project over the windows—in fact, since the windows are, as a rule,

* Formerly known as the Girls' Institute.

flush with the wall, they admit a maximum quantity of light.

We may conclude our consideration of the architecture as follows: Some nine out of ten cottages are pretty and pleasant to live in, the remaining one being invariably, both as regards beauty and convenience, far above the average working man's cottage. Building has lately been stopped, but, when it is resumed, it is almost certain that experience will have taught the estate office which are the most successful schemes, so that the proportion of failures will ultimately be reduced below even the present modest proportion. As some of the cottages are almost twenty years old, and as they have been built at different dates, there is at Port Sunlight an opportunity of studying the results of weathering. In most cases they are excellent, particularly as regards the brickwork and the yellow roughcast; these somewhat assertive materials are toning down, though at a slower rate than they would in an industrial city. I am not prepared to regret it, for our great towns grow gloomy far too soon. As it is, many of the cottages, particularly those built with plaster and sunken beams, have lost their suggestion of newness; they have become homes in the best sense, for so long as the house is new it is not a home but only a dwelling.

The final conclusion as regards the general effect is that it depends to a great extent on circumstances other than architecture; Port Sunlight without its spirit would be only an ideal mushroom city, an antiseptic paradise. Of this I shall have more to say further on, but I cannot pass over the fact that the extreme cleanliness of the house-fronts, the complete

COTTAGES.

COTTAGES.

[*To face p.* 70.

absence of refuse, the unbroken panes, the tidy white curtains, and the trim creepers go a long way towards making Port Sunlight what it is. The creepers are a feature the importance of which would only be realized if they were removed; they are sturdily invading every wall and even the roofs: some of the cottages are already heavily laden with ivy, virginia creeper, and other climbing plants that burst into flower as the year ripens. They are the special care of the estate, and, in fact, it seems almost impossible to traverse Port Sunlight without encountering the gardeners perpetually clipping and trimming; so much so that the close-cropped foliage reminds us irresistibly of the wooden trees that once emerged from our Nuremberg playboxes. The Port Sunlight secret lies in the tree and the shrub, but still more in the broad meadow; the houses are generally built on one side of the road only and overlook broad spaces of grass or belts of trees. This increases the feeling of privacy—a feeling which has its moral value so long as it is not allowed to destroy the social spirit.

The influence of Port Sunlight on the district has, strange to say, been small. At Bebington there is a large Roman Catholic School, built in 1903, the architecture of which recalls that of the Village, but beyond finding this instance I explored New Ferry and Bebington in vain. In both these little places the defects that have become familiar to us are apparent. Bebington is still semi-rural and has, I expect, pleasant spots, but the most pleasant of them will not long escape the righteous wrath of the sanitary authorities, whilst the newer parts are built on the familiar square brick box pattern. New Ferry is still worse, for it is entirely urban; row after row of brick cottages, of pretentious stucco-fronted villas, and blocks of brand new "workmen's" cottages which will be slum property within twenty years; this sums up the neighbourhood. It is truly a wonderful and awful contrast; if we follow the Chester Road, for instance, going towards Birkenhead, we find on the one side the Port Sunlight cottages, graceful and clean, with trim gardens in front; on the other the houses of New Ferry, dirty, monotonous, and unspeakably ugly, fronted by small yards often choked with rubbish. Here and there a dark and frowsy shop and, still worse, the ever-present low-class public-house, the existence of which we had almost forgotten. Truly, nothing reads so clear a lesson as does this comparison!

THE FIVE-ROOM STANDARD.—Let us, however, forget, if we can, the surrounding ugliness and return to the Village to study more closely the house itself. The Port Sunlight cottages are of two classes, the kitchen and the parlour type. The kitchen house comprises a kitchen (with scullery and pantry), which is used as a living room and takes in most of the ground floor, three bedrooms, and a bathroom fitted with hot and cold water taps; in the parlour house there is a large living room, a kitchen with scullery and pantry, four bedrooms, and a bathroom. It should be noted, for this is very important, that no house has less than five rooms,* three of which are bedrooms, because this raises social questions of the highest importance.

* Except half a dozen three-roomed cottages which are being used by old or childless couples or by pensioners.

COTTAGES.

COTTAGES. [*To face p.* 72.

If the Port Sunlight system is to solve the housing problem, it will be because it has accepted and exceeded the four-room standard, without which it is difficult for a family to be brought up, I do not say under good sanitary conditions, because that is admittedly impossible, but in such a manner as to fit its members to take their place among those that are clean in mind and soul. We have often been harrowed by the description of what happens in our big cities, of the families herded in two rooms, even in one room—of four, five, six, even ten adults and children owning but a single room, in which they must live, eat, sleep, and even wash if such an inclination survive the conditions. It is not necessary to go so far; it is true that the census of 1901 tells us that in London alone there were 148,000 persons living in 40,600 rooms, or an average of between three and four persons per room, and it can hardly be necessary to show once more that under such circumstances there can be no hope of happiness for the miserable tenement dwellers. Their fate is to be subjected from their childhood upwards to the foulest temptations and examples, to be herded together irrespective of age or sex, untaught and unshepherded, to be taunted in after years with their moral degradation by the middle-class authors of their misery. We know or should realize that at the root of all forms of vice, particularly drunkenness, lies the problem of housing; evil conditions mean depression, and, for the slag of our social system, the only resource, fleeting but efficacious, is the public-house and its costly hospitality.

GOOD HOUSING AS A MORAL INFLUENCE.—We

are often told that the working man is drunken, thriftless, and immoral; I will not deny it, but who will say that the changeling son of a duke would withstand the influences that so often make the child of the unskilled labourer what he is? But let it not be forgotten, these are our brethren, and the greater their degradation the greater are both our guilt and our duty. This case needs no pleading; but the horror of the housing question, for those who have come into contact with it, lies in the ignorance and the unconscious cruelty of the classes, of those well-meaning but un-understanding and hopelessly warped men and women who think that the woes of the English people can be cured either by the district visitor or the Kyrle Society. The pictures of our city slums rise before our eyes, and it is difficult to argue coldly and logically, so violent is the gust of passion that overwhelms one who can picture the slum family: the man hopelessly brutalized because he has no "home," because he is driven into the wet streets or the glaring gin shop by the noise and the dirt; the woman, old at thirty and her girlish beauty gone, shrewish, over-worked, her nerves jarred by continual association with the children, by her life in the foul atmosphere of the kitchen and the washtub; the children feeble, ill fed, herded together in one room, often in one bed, deprived of air, of food, of light, and rich only in the vicious experience that oozes from the very pavements of our great cities.

There is one way and only one way of coping with drunkenness, immorality, ignorance, crime, with everything that we call evil, and that is good housing. And good housing means as an irreducible minimum two

COTTAGES.

COTTAGES. [*To face p.* 74.

rooms for a married couple, three rooms if they have not more than two children of one sex, four rooms if their children be of different sexes, and never less than one room for every two persons. Generally speaking, therefore, a four-roomed house is the *minimum*. In urban tenements all the rooms are used as bedrooms, but this is not satisfactory; let any middle-class man who has any doubts on this point consider whether he could contemplate doing without his dining-room and his drawing-room. The three-bedroom standard is, therefore, a *minimum* where there is a family of boys and girls; two rooms are useless, though it has seriously been suggested that the father and sons should occupy one of the bedrooms, the mother and daughters the other. This is an absurd solution, and I do not suppose that, in the present state of human opinion, it would endure very long if established. The demand is therefore: a bedroom for the parents, one for the boys and one for the girls; we cannot very well find an argument against this arrangement, for a lodger can always be introduced if all the rooms are not occupied. It will be seen further on, in the rules that regulate tenancies, how carefully this question is dealt with, but I do not think it worth while to expatiate on this four-room standard; it is one which we can take for granted, and it is not a *maximum* but a *minimum*; we do not now ask for marble halls for the worker, but there is no reason why he should not live in decent comfort.

Whether we have to deal with the "kitchen house" of five rooms, or the "parlour house" of six rooms, the features of the Port Sunlight cottage are substantially the same. The houses vary but little in appearance; they are neither more nor less ornate; in fact, it is difficult to tell the parlour house from the kitchen house until one enters it. Otherwise, particularly as regards the important adjuncts—scullery, pantry, and bathroom—there is but little to choose between the houses; the difference lies to a certain extent in space, though the kitchen is sometimes as large as the parlour, but mainly in the use that is made of it. The average frontage of a Port Sunlight cottage is eighteen feet, and the dimensions of the front room (whether it be a parlour or a kitchen) are not, as a rule, less than fourteen feet by twelve, and often fourteen by fourteen. That is a good room, and the scullery at the back is always sufficiently large to rid the kitchen during the day of the grosser evidences of cooking. If we pass through this scullery we note that, in all the houses, a copper has been fitted; it has a movable lid, so that the apparatus does not only expedite operations on washing-day, but it serves as a table at other times. Behind the scullery is a ventilated larder; the room also contains a sink provided nowadays with both hot and cold water taps. Behind the scullery is the back-yard, paved with brick and sloping well away from the house, with the offices not less than seven feet from the cottage.

In the smaller houses there is no hall, but only a passage; in the parlour houses this room is fully equal to its equivalent in a London block of flats. On the first floor we find either three or four bedrooms, according to the size of the house; one is large and the others small, often rather too small, though it is, of course, better, for the reasons already given, that a large family should have several small rooms rather

THORNTON HOUGH.

THICKETFORD (THORNTON HOUGH). [*To face p.* 76.

than few large ones. The bedrooms all have flat ceilings; they are not attic built. This secures abundance of light and air. I may add, in this connection, that wherever a room has no fireplace a ventilator has been fixed, though I grieve to say that even in Port Sunlight I found one or two of these stuffed with rags, and a few windows nailed up; to teach the people hygiene is no easy matter. The difficulty of ventilation is met, however, by the comparatively large size of the smallest rooms, viz. twelve feet by nine by eight, or eight hundred and sixty-four cubic feet: a minimum of ventilation will maintain good conditions in such a room if it be occupied by but one person.

All these rooms are exceedingly open and well lighted; the entire front of the living room is usually cut away and replaced by casement windows, with or without a bay window, all opening outwards. The bedrooms have narrow but very high windows in the same style; the best bedroom has, as a rule, two large windows, but does not repeat the bay window of the ground floor. This is worth noting, owing to the prevalence in London suburbs of an architectural heresy, the piling one upon the other of two, three, and even more bay windows, the process being repeated along the entire length of a road, which apparently goes on for ever.

A few details that could not be classed should be added. Every house has its own dustbin, which is emptied by the Council employees; sewage of all sorts is dealt with by the Urban District Council, and is very easily disposed of, thanks to the ebb tide of the Mersey. Water is provided by a private company—the West Cheshire. Gas is laid on in every cottage, and is retailed by meter. There are no basements in Port Sunlight—an excellent rule against which no protests have been made; sunken portions, such as the coal cellar, are outside the house. The cottages are well provided with fittings. In the kitchen is an elaborate range, supplemented sometimes by a small gas stove; there are also cupboards, both in the kitchen and upstairs; hat and coat rails are fixed in the hall, and gas-fittings for the whole house are supplied free. These are rather important items for working-class families who, as a rule, find it inconvenient to expend much on fixtures, owing to the fluctuating nature of their employment.

It is difficult to generalize in these matters, but it is safe to say that, taking them all round, the cottages are the best possible for a working man. When he has a small family, the kitchen house, with its good living room and three bedrooms, is ideal; but if he has five or six children this type is very inconvenient, nor does he gain very much in sleeping accommodation if he can afford the rent of a parlour house. In neither case is there, of course, any question of overcrowding: there is no overcrowding at Port Sunlight as we understand the word. The census basis, for instance, would fix as a limit for the five-roomed house * eight adults or as many adults and children (counted as half an adult) as would make up a total of eight adults; for instance, three adults (over sixteen) and ten children would not exceed the limit, and the fact that the cold official view of overcrowding accepts such a standard shows what must be the

* Deducting one room for bathroom, hall and scullery combined.

COTTAGES. [*To face p.* 78.

terrible condition of urban housing. In the parlour house we find four bedrooms, but two are always small, so that difficulties present themselves; but I suppose that under the present social system difficulties cannot be avoided as regards the housing of the working class. It seems, however, that there is room for a third type of house, which I might call the "family cottage," consisting of a large kitchen and living room combined, a small bedroom occupying the remainder of the ground floor. The first floor could then either be divided into four rooms, as is now the case, or, better still, into three, when their size would become such as to allow of each being occupied by two persons. Moreover, a room should be something more than a sleeping place, viz. a refuge from noise and society; co-operation and mutual intercourse must not be discouraged; but they must not be forced upon the people, and it is important that all the members of a family should have opportunities for reading and thinking in private.

These are, however, small matters, and one is almost ashamed to venture upon counselling perfection to the organizers of a village which approaches more nearly than any other system that perfection of housing that can alone make life worth living; I feel quite sure that the perusal of the following chapters, particularly that which deals with the Village institutions, will prove beyond doubt that the objects of the scheme—health, education, and sociability—have been realized to the full.

CHAPTER V

THE VILLAGE: ECONOMIC CONDITIONS

PORT SUNLIGHT is not an open estate; it is an experiment in model housing in the same way as Earswick and Garden City, but in so far as it aims at directly influencing the Factory workers it is also something more. So long as it does not and cannot accommodate them all, it is absolutely necessary, if the object of the scheme is to be attained, to confine its benefits to the employees of the Works. Hard things have been said of the Village as regards this aspect of the question; it has been stated, or more or less plainly hinted, that Port Sunlight does not come up to the standard of other model villages because it is "bounty fed." This is a doctrinaire view, or rather, it shows a lack of comprehension of the aims of the founders; it is true that Port Sunlight rents are low, in fact, uncommercial *qua* rents, but in this fact lies the very essence of the scheme, viz. profit-sharing or prosperity-sharing. This question is so fully dealt with in another chapter that it is unnecessary to consider it here, but it must be admitted that it is both legitimate and sensible to restrict the benefits conferred on the residents to the employees of the Works. If Port Sunlight could accommodate all its workers and

COTTAGES. [*To face p.* 80.

their families, then, if outsiders were admitted on an unprofitable scale, it would be time to cry out "bounties," but that is very far from being the case at present.

The Village consists of seven hundred and twenty houses, and of these about seven hundred are occupied by employees of Messrs. Lever Brothers, or of Village institutions. The remaining twenty are held either by former employees, or by outsiders who are specially authorized; it will be seen that, to all intents and purposes, the Village is closely preserved for the employees. The rules for tenants being short and explicit, they may be quoted in full—

RULES FOR THE REGULATION OF TENANCIES ON THE PORT SUNLIGHT ESTATE.

RULE 1.—Persons to be eligible for dwellings must have their applications approved by the directors of Lever Brothers Limited. Priority will be given to those engaged on the permanent staff in offices and works of the Company, or in institutions in Port Sunlight, but in specially approved cases other applicants for houses may be admitted subject to payment of an increased rent of $33\frac{1}{3}$ per cent.

RULE 2.—The tenancies are from week to week.

RULE 3.—No tenant may sub-let his house or part of it.

RULE 4.—Tenants desirous of having lodgers must have themselves registered at the offices of the Company as so desirous, and each lodger's name and occupation must be handed into the office by the tenant. Lodger's date of entry and date of leaving must also be supplied.

RULE 5.—No one may lodge in the Village who is not in the employment of the Company, or their sub-contractors.

RULE 6.—Lodgers in one house must be of the same sex.

RULE 7.—The following regulations respecting lodgers will be strictly enforced :—

> "Tenants with families of more than two children, or with children over twelve years of age, must not keep lodgers. Tenants with one or two children under twelve years of age may keep one lodger. Tenants without families may keep two lodgers." (See Note.)

RULE 8.—An authorized official of the Company may visit any house in Port Sunlight, at any time, for the purpose of seeing that due regard is being paid to order and cleanliness.

RULE 9.—The tenant is liable for all loss by broken windows and internal damages (fair wear and tear excepted), which he must make good or pay for on giving up possession.

RULE 10.—In order to maintain the health and cleanliness of the Village, no tenant will be allowed to keep poultry, or to erect poultry houses or similar erections, in the yards of the cottages, but tenants may keep poultry in the allotment gardens, provided they create no nuisance.

RULE 11.—In the case of infectious disease in any house on the estate, tenants are required to *at once* notify the same to the Company's office or estate office.

NOTE.—"Lodger" to be understood to mean any person not being the father or mother or child of tenant. Married sons or daughters (and their wives or husbands) will be considered as "lodgers."

It will be seen from Rule 1 that an employee is not entitled to be housed, but that he has priority. The object of this rule is to provide as much as possible for those whose occupation at the Works is permanent. It has not been thought advisable, since accommodation is limited, to admit tenants

COTTAGES. [*To face p.* 82.

strictly in order of priority of application, for this would let in the casual and semi-casual element, and entail upon the estate expenses in repairs and cleaning which would ultimately react unfavourably upon the rents.

Rule 2 is important because it has been the cause of a good deal of controversy. When an employee leaves the Works, or is discharged, he receives at the same time notice to give up his house within a week, but this notice is not often enforced. It is obvious on the one hand that the problem facing a man who has just lost his employment is seriously complicated by his having to find another home, for it interferes with his far more important search for work. On the other hand, given that a large number of men are engaged at the Works, and that continual fluctuations are inevitable, it is clear that, if tenants were allowed to retain possession of their houses indefinitely after having left the Factory, the Village would by degrees pass into the hands of outsiders; the objects of the scheme would be frustrated, and non-employees would draw a bonus in the shape of improved housing at a low rate, to which the workers at the Factory are alone entitled. This difficulty has, however, been recognized by the estate, and I understand that it is not now usual to press the notice to quit, but that tenants are, as a rule, allowed a month in which to vacate their cottages. The estate reserves to itself full control of this extension, for it is clearly justified in refusing to afford facilities when, for instance, a man has been dismissed for dishonesty. On the other hand, it is not good that arbitrary power of this nature should be vested in the hands of minor officials, whose action may easily become vexatious; this, however, is a matter of administration.

The rules concerning lodgers show on the one hand that the authorities are determined to keep up the moral tone of the Village, and on the other, that overcrowding is not to be allowed to nullify the value of the general scheme. This particular question is notoriously serious in all our great cities; the lodger is usually a young man from the country, or, in the poorer parts, a casual labourer without a family; in many cases lodgers are admitted into tenements which are already overcrowded, and share both sleeping and living rooms with the family. It does not need very much knowledge or even imagination to realize that this practice does not make for a high moral standard; indeed, the perils of admitting a stranger so closely into the family circle are obvious and notorious; every night and in every music hall in England this subject is alluded to in a would-be jocular manner, but it is quite clear that domestic trouble of the most detestable kind, or even more painful acceptance of facts, should be stringently guarded against. I do not, therefore, think that Rules 4, 5, 6, and 7 can arouse much opposition.

Rule 8 is worth noting because the work of the authorized official has become almost a sinecure; the fact is obvious after one has visited some half-dozen homes, and realized to how great an extent the rule has affected the tenants' mode of living. The provisions may appear vexatious, but it is not really more so than the visit of the sanitary or school attendance officer; at any rate, I did not hear any complaints on this score.

The object of Rule 10 is stated in the text; pigs may not be kept at all, which is perhaps unfortunate, but it would be difficult to do so satisfactorily on the ten perches of an allotment; poultry and pigeons are, however, kept there in numbers, so that the rule does not interfere unduly with the comfort of the tenants.

These are not stringent rules, except as regards the lodger question, but they could well be made more severe if it were desired to counterbalance the considerable advantages derived by the tenants in the shape of low rents. Beautiful and comfortable homes are admittedly important, but, before all things, if we are to solve the housing problem, we need cheap homes, low rents. Strictly speaking, Port Sunlight rents are not very low, if we take into consideration the "prosperity-sharing" which modifies them. It is rather difficult to arrive at a figure which would be the legitimate rent of a Port Sunlight cottage. The average price of land, originally £240 per acre, has been increased by additions and by local betterment; the cost of the cottages varies a great deal, as much as 50 per cent., if we compare the smallest kitchen house with the largest parlour house; the cost has varied considerably even inside each class with the accommodation and especially the decoration. Roughly speaking, if we take the ultimate figure of building at ten cottages to the acre and the land at the very moderate price of £300 per acre, we find that each cottage accounts for a capital value of £30 per site; this figure is not likely to decrease: it is far from over-estimated as it is. As regards the cost of cottages, the kitchen house averages £275, and the parlour house £375; some of the later types of both classes have reached £300 and £400, the plaster and sunken beam cottage being the most costly.

The above figures are interesting, but they are quoted only in view of the agitation that has been carried on for some years in favour of "cheap" cottages. The cost is certainly rather high; the Urban Cottages Exhibition at Letchworth in 1907 showed that a house of the "Kitchen" type could be built, if not for £200, as was desired, at any rate for £225, and a "Parlour" house for £265. They were all, it is true, much less ornate and some less substantial than Port Sunlight cottages, and their cost did not include yard walls, architects' fees, cartage, etc., but still there is a difference. It should be said that it was not desired, at Port Sunlight, to cut prices to any great extent, and the comparison is in no wise derogatory, for the object of the Letchworth exhibition was to show what could be done at a minimum cost, whilst the founders of Port Sunlight set out to attain an ideal with a comparative disregard of cost, and above all to build beautiful houses for the people; many cottages bear the addition of £50 for bay windows, gables, etc. At Earswick also, Mr. Rowntree's model village, the cost of a kitchen house is well below the Port Sunlight figure, but far less has been spent on beautifying the frontages. It must therefore be understood that Port Sunlight is an experiment rather in ideal than in cheap housing.

PORT SUNLIGHT RENTALS.—The rentals are, however, not unduly heavy. The kitchen houses are let at prices varying between 3*s.* 6*d.* and 4*s.* 6*d.*, according to size of rooms and situation, to which should be added 1*s.* 6*d.* to 1*s.* 9*d.* for rates, making the gross rentals 5*s.* to 6*s.* 3*d.* per week. The parlour houses are let at 5*s.* 6*d.*, 6*s.* 6*d.*, and 7*s.* 6*d.*, amounts which are brought up by rates to 7*s.* 6*d.*, 8*s.* 9*d.*, and 10*s.* From these figures, taking the commonest type of both classes, we see that the average rent is about 5*s.* 9*d.* per week for a kitchen house and 8*s.* 9*d.* for a parlour house, including rates and repairs; most of the factory workers live in cottages rented at less than 6*s.* per week, the larger houses being occupied mainly by foremen, skilled artisans, and clerks.

These rentals absorb, on an average, between one-quarter and one-fifth of the worker's weekly wage; this is, of course, far too large a proportion, but one that is unfortunately too frequent everywhere. Indeed, particularly in London, it is usual to find the workman paying as much for a two-roomed tenement as he does in Port Sunlight for an entire cottage; so there is no doubt that, taking things not as they should be, but as they are, he is getting far more for his money than he would anywhere else. Evidence of this is not lacking; in Birkenhead and Liverpool it is impossible to obtain in working-class neighbourhoods surroundings and sanitation to equal those of Port Sunlight, and yet the nearest equivalent costs the workman about one-third more than it would on the estate. When the experiment of admitting outsiders was tried the estate office was flooded with applications, in spite of the fact that outsiders were charged one-third extra; as it is, some twenty outsiders contentedly pay these very much enhanced rents for the privilege of living in the Village, though their work lies outside its boundaries.

RATES AT PORT SUNLIGHT.—The attraction of Port Sunlight lies, not only in its low rents, but in the fact that far higher rents do not command similar accommodation in the neighbourhood. This has been recognized in a manner not altogether pleasant for the villagers, the urban district council having for many years assessed the cottages above their rental basis; thus not only is no abatement allowed, but a cottage the net rent of which is 4*s.* 3*d.* may, for the purposes of rating, be assessed at 5*s.* This is not unfair, for the authorities must take into consideration the peculiar scheme of profit-sharing which influences the rental figure; the upshot is that Port Sunlight carries a burden of rates which is not counterbalanced by its political power. In 1907 the five wards of the Lower Bebington Urban District numbered 1946 electors, out of whom Port Sunlight accounted for 586. Out of eighteen members of the Council Port Sunlight returned five, or 30 per cent., while paying 50 per cent. of the local rates. I do not for a moment suggest that voting power should absolutely follow the purse, but in local affairs it has generally been assumed that he who pays must rule, and when the disproportion between obligations and rights is so great as it is in this instance, there appears to be room for a readjustment of wards. In the case of Lower Bebington U.D.C., there is beyond doubt room for redistribution; Bebington ward, for instance, with 343 voters, returns six members, and Port Sunlight ward, with 374 voters, has only three.

On the basis of population, therefore, as well as of rates, representation no longer corresponds to conditions; in view of the similar position in which

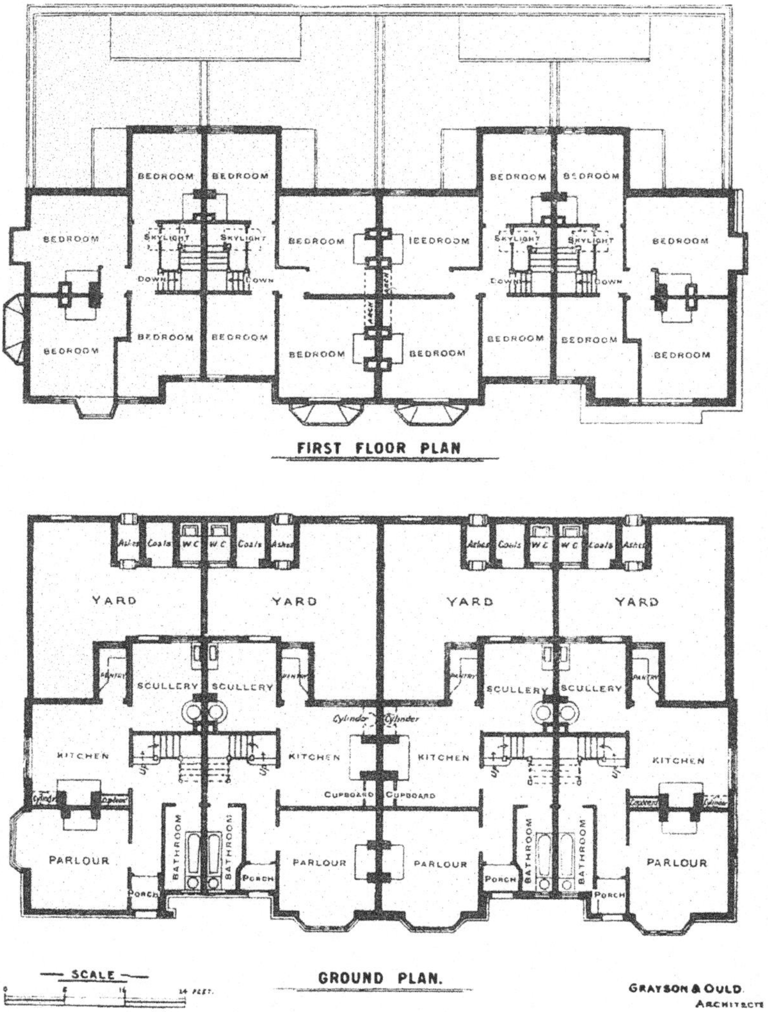

PARLOUR COTTAGES, PORT SUNLIGHT

[*To face p.* 88.

Parliament itself has been ever since it became "representative," I suppose it is too much to hope for an amendment of these conditions.

HOW RATES ARE PAID.—Each tenant authorizes the Company to deduct from the wages a weekly instalment towards payment of rates. When he receives his rate-demand note, he brings it to the Company, who supply the necessary funds from the tenant's own rates account. In effect, the firm conduct what may be called a Savings Bank for rates. The cost of collection is in this way materially reduced, as collectors have only to make one call. The tenant being in communication with the local authority, is able to realize that administration is or is not efficient. His interest in local government is quickened. This interest is, as a rule, lukewarm enough, as is shown by the polling returns in English towns; a 50 per cent. poll is far from bad, and the proportion is often lower. At Port Sunlight the effect of this system has been to increase popular interest in local questions, which affect the householder to a far greater extent than do imperial questions, and it would certainly be desirable to establish it everywhere.

THE VILLAGE ACCOUNT.—Apart from variations in the rates, which are neither large nor frequent, the Port Sunlight rents have been influenced of late years by the state of the Village account. As I have already hinted, the principle of the scheme is set forth in another chapter, but it is necessary to outline it here because it influences the rents. The capital cost of the Village, including land, cottages, open spaces, public buildings, institutions, etc., is taken at a lump sum, about £500,000; on this capital value 5 per cent.

interest is charged by the Company, or about £25,000. To this sum we must add 1 per cent. depreciation on buildings, upkeep and repairs, cost of estate administration, etc. It should be said that the interest charge of £25,000 is returned to the Village account by the Company as a profit-sharing contribution; thus it is only a *pro forma* entry and does not actually affect the rents. These have, however, fluctuated to a certain extent, and they are now higher than they were in the beginning; this is in part due to the exaggerated demands for repairs that are made by the tenants. The landlord having contracted to undertake repairs as well as to keep up the gardens, the tenants are naturally more inclined to make such demands than if they had to defray these expenses out of their own pockets. In the long run they suffer indirectly, for the body of tenants is its own landlord in so far as its expenditure tends to fix the standard of rents. The outlook is, however, improving, for the tenants have begun to realize that individual extravagance reacts unfavourably upon the comfort of the community; the result of this growing feeling is something more important than diminishing rents: solidarity and a tendency towards social co-operation.

Apart from the question of high or low rents, it seems essential that the Village account should be so balanced as to make variation impossible. Fluctuating rents are as bad as fluctuating bonuses; they amount to almost exactly the same thing and their results are equally serious. A drop in the rent rarely means that thrift will be encouraged; I do not suggest that the difference will necessarily be dissipated, but it is

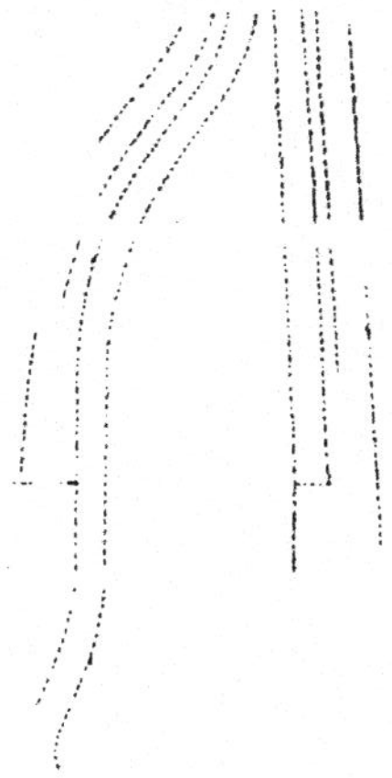

COTTAGES, PORT SUNLIGHT.

SECTION

SCALE

0 8 16 24 FEET

more likely to be expended on luxuries than on necessaries; thus, when rents rise once more, the tenant finds himself face to face with reduced means and increased desires. The rents must be as nearly fixed as is humanly possible. Of course the cry among the Port Sunlight tenants is for further reductions, and the demand is quite understandable, but it would be imprudent to yield to it at present. Even when the Village account has taken over the upkeep of all the institutions and has a balance on the right side, rents should not be reduced at once; it will be necessary to accumulate a reserve capable of coping with a succession of, say seven, bad years, which is a little more than the average duration of a complete commercial crisis. A conservative policy of this kind is bound to create discontent, but it would be criminal to jeopardize in cold blood the success of so promising a scheme. I do not doubt that the growing sense of solidarity among the tenants will soon allow of the Village account taking over the institutions in their entirety; as it is, the last yearly accounts show a credit balance of over £1000.

Generally speaking, the tenants have nothing but good words to say for the system and its administrators, but there are a few complaints. Over and above the rent question, which could hardly be settled unless its amount were brought down to vanishing point, there is a feeling that the Company should defray the upkeep and expenses of the institutions; it will be seen in Chapter VI. how these are controlled, and I believe that the reader will agree that the institutions are as favoured by the Company as is good for them. The institutions already enjoy the great advantage of being provided with buildings at a low cost, and it is notorious that an organized body which is not extensively supported by its members inevitably becomes a hotbed of patronage. It would be better that the institutions should become extinct than that they should lose their independence. There are also the usual complaints against certain officials, some of which are probably well- and some ill-founded; it would be futile to enter into the details of complex cases, for they do not bear upon the principles of the scheme. It may be taken, therefore, that, on the whole, the tenants are well satisfied with housing conditions.

Before dismissing the subject of the Village itself, the "Village Account," to which I have referred before now, should be analyzed in greater detail. Strictly speaking, it should be called the "Village Accounts," for it comprises a memorandum of capital outlay and a statement of the income and expenditure; when used in the singular the words usually refer to the latter. Both these documents, made up to December 31, 1907, are reproduced here, for it is impossible otherwise to gain a clear idea of the state of the Village finances.

PORT SUNLIGHT VILLAGE

MEMORANDA OF CAPITAL OUTLAY AND MAINTENANCE ACCOUNT.

(1) CAPITAL OUTLAY, DECEMBER 31, 1907.

	£ s. d.	£ s. d.
Purchase of 132 acres of Land, Making of Roads, Drainage, Levelling and Filling in Pool, Laying of Mains, and Erection of Bridges ..		137,178 10 0
Erection of Cottages, Shops, and Bridge Inn	282,726 4 6	
Furniture in the Bridge Inn ..	1,826 3 0	
		284,552 7 6
Laying-out of Parks, Gardens, Bowling-green, Rifle-range, Recreation Grounds, and Part Cost of Football Enclosure		8,047 10 7
Schools (Park Road and Church Drive) and Cost of Extension of the Technical Institute previously presented to Village	29,973 0 3	
Furniture and Fittings contained in above	3,428 8 1	
		33,401 8 4
Auditorium, Baths, Band Stand, Collegium, Gymnasium, Hospital, Library, and Social and Bowling Club	29,745 15 3	
Furniture contained in the above, together with the Band Instruments	5,599 18 8	
		35,345 13 11
Church .. .. (a Gift)	—	—
Technical Institute .. (a Gift)		—
		£498,525 10 4

(2) MAINTENANCE

INCOME.

	£	s.	d.
Rents of Cottages, Shops, Bridge Inn, and Allotment Gardens	8,490	9	11
Interest as above allowed by Lever Brothers Limited	24,680	10	7
	£33,171	0	6

ACCOUNT, 1907.

EXPENDITURE.

	£	s.	d.
Cottages and Bridge Inn—Repairs, Beautifying, and Sundries	1,617	13	5
Upkeep of Parks, Gardens, and Walks	471	16	7
Deficits on Working Accounts, Sundry Repairs, Alterations and payments in connection with— Schools and Technical Institute .. .. .. Auditorium, Baths, Band, Collegium, Cottage Hospital, Football Club, Gymnasium, Library, Musical Expenses, Social and Bowling Club ..	647	0	1
Office Expenses—			
Salary and Wages	366	8	6
Printing, Postages, and Sundries	27	7	11
General Expenses—			
Depreciation (Basis:—1% on Buildings, 7½% on Furniture, per annum)	4,150	0	0
Interest (Basis : — 5% on Capital Outlay, December 31, 1906	24,680	10	7
Insurance	158	4	6
Tithe Rent	9	7	10
Christ Church—Expenses and Salaries of Minister, Lay Helper, Choir, etc., are not charged in this Account, being met by proceeds from Pew Rents, Collections, and Voluntary Contributions.			
	£32,128	9	5

SUMMARY—Years 1902–7 (excluding Interest on Capital Outlay).

	£	s.	d.
Balance, a deficiency from last account..	2055	11	4
Deduct surplus for 1907, as above	1042	11	1
Balance to next account	£1013	0	3
Surplus for year, excluding Interest on Capital Outlay	1042	11	1

COTTAGES.

[*To face p.* 96.

The above accounts are certainly clear and comprehensive, and call for little remark. It will be observed that the price of the Village land works out at over £1000 an acre, as opposed to the £240 quoted in the early part of this chapter; the difference is traceable partly to the enhanced cost of the additional land that was bought (a testimony to the improvement of ground values in the district), but mainly to the cost of transforming the older part of the estate into an inhabitable district.

The cost of the cottages is also interesting; if we allow for Bridge Inn and the extra expenditure on shops, we find that the 720 houses in Port Sunlight cost on an average about £385 each; this bears out the calculations made in the early part of this chapter, and is worthy of notice though it does not take into account the two types, kitchen and parlour houses.

The schools have, on the whole, been very cheap; their cost works out at £23 10*s*. per school place, which is not in itself low, but if we take into account their spaciousness and beauty we cannot but think that their price is very moderate indeed. It is enough to recall that the total capital outlay amounts to close on £500,000, and to point out that the church and the technical institute are not included in this figure before we pass on to the far more important and interesting maintenance account.

The income and expenditure account is the test, and by it the scheme must stand or fall: either it can pay its way and thus justify its existence or it can do no better than accumulate deficit on deficit and so brand the enterprise as a failure. Let us, therefore, examine the items with care. The first is that of repairs. These account for over £1600; as beautifying is nowadays a small matter it is beyond doubt too high. I have stated above the dilemma in which the Company was placed: it had either to leave the repairs to the tenants and endanger the beauty of the Village or undertake them itself and see them increase. The second alternative has been accepted, and, I think, rightly; even if the tenants do not for many years complete their education in solidarity, an education which will make them realize that their economies and those of their neighbours are all for the common good, it is important to preserve for the Village its external beauty. Besides, the inhabitants are beginning to realize how much scope there is for a reduction in repairs; at present they amount to almost 20 per cent. of the rent roll, a figure which any estate agent will agree is extremely high: with the facilities that exist in the Works for an organization on a large scale it should be about 10 per cent. A reduction of this item to its proper level will make for a great improvement in the Village accounts, and when these are in a sufficiently strong position will allow a reduction in the rents of *6d.* to *9d.* per week.

The upkeep of parks, gardens, schools, institute, and of certain Village institutions amounts altogether to £1119; this is not a very large figure, but it is likely to increase somewhat later on. As the finances of the Village improve, the other institutions, such as the Collegium,* will become dependent on this account; it is important that the Village should become entirely self-supporting, and it is therefore desirable that every expense connected with its upkeep should be defrayed

* Formerly Girls' Institute.

before there is any talk of reduction of rents. The outlook as regards this question is dealt with in Chapter X., as is also the contribution of £24,680 10*s.* 7*d.* As regards depreciation it is enough to note that the estimates are prudent, for the account provides for amortization of the capital cost of the houses within one hundred years, and of the furniture within ten years; there is every reason to expect that another decade or so will show that the cost of the houses is being fully redeemed, and this will strengthen the position still further.

The upshot of the foregoing analysis is, therefore, that last year showed a profit on maintenance account of over £1000, and that the deficiency resulting from the last five years' working has been reduced to a little over £1000; thus the probability is that at the end of 1908 the Village account will show a credit balance. It is already self-supporting, and it will then be in a position to improve still further the lot of the tenants. I assume, of course, that the "interest contribution" is permanent, for it modifies the rents to a large extent. If the Village were to be kept up exactly as it is, repay capital and interest, etc., the rents would have to be raised, but this, of course, is not a commercial proposition, for it would frustrate the essential objects of the scheme.

As it is, however, the Village may be considered as self-supporting, and I do not think that it is ever likely to become a further charge upon the funds of the Company. Indeed, if more houses are built, its success is likely to be still greater, for fixed charges will then be spread over a larger rent roll, and the Village institutions will become independent of the parent account. At present the Village is growing, as it has done from the beginning. Though the increases of population in the last two or three years do not absolutely correspond to an increase in houseroom, they are a fair index of the growth of the Village.

Year	Estimated population
1900	2007
1901	2331
1902	2484
1903	2580
1904	2610
1905	2700
1906	2900
1907	3600

It will be seen that the population has increased in seven years by exactly 50 per cent., which is far from unsatisfactory. In view of the number of applications received by the estate office, it will probably be necessary very soon to resume building operations, when we may expect the population to increase at a still more rapid rate; at present all vacant houses are applied for, and it is rare that they remain empty longer than a fortnight, which is sufficient testimony to their popularity.

ALLOTMENTS.—Before dismissing the Village itself reference should be made to that feature which enables us to class it specifically among the garden cities, viz. allotments for the inhabitants. These little plots, of which there are but too few in country districts (about one million acres altogether in the United Kingdom in plots smaller than one acre), are practically unknown in little towns of three thousand and six

ALLOTMENT GARDENS.

[*To face p.* 100.

hundred inhabitants. At Port Sunlight the importance of affording scope for healthful, as well as remunerative, employment of the people's leisure has not been lost sight of. There is a good deal of vacant land, and most of it will not be built on, either because it is on too steep a slope or because the proportion of building to open land must be maintained; the dells and the central portions of the building sections are ideally suited for allotments. It is now hardly necessary to defend the view that labour on the land is a healthful change for a man who is confined during the day within a factory, however well ventilated it may be. It may be said that he will be too tired to do much work in addition to his daily eight hours, but experience shows that rest is found in change rather than in idleness; at any rate, the Sunlighters do not appear to despise allotments as a form of recreation, for at the time of my last visit there was hardly a vacant plot.

Allotments are granted by the estate at the rate of ten perches for every householder, and those who have the leisure to cultivate a larger area may have a double plot. In some cases men who have large families are well able, with the help of their children, to run twenty perches, and it is perhaps in the influence of agricultural work upon the children that the essential value of the scheme may be found. The allotments are let on a commercial basis, at the rate of 5*s.* per annum, including water for irrigation, which costs 2*s.* 6*d.* per allotment; this brings out the net rent per acre at about £2 per annum. Yet there is evidence that the margin of profit is adequate, for no less than two hundred and fifty men have taken up land, a considerable number in a village of seven hundred and twenty houses. It is difficult to say what the average gross yield is, but most of the plots produce £4 to £5 per annum, some as much as £7 or £8 where early vegetables are raised under glass, and a few, the occupiers of which grow flowers, a good deal more. Thus most of the allotment holders make as much as *2s.* a week (labour being recreation); these weekly two shillings have their importance in such small budgets as those of the Sunlighters, especially as this money is earned in kind, and is therefore a generous two shillings worth; moreover, it is earned by pleasant employment of leisure time, and by forswearing more costly amusements. The labour entailed by an allotment amounts to about two hours per diem from March to September, and a day a month during the winter. Profits are increased in many cases by poultry and bee-keeping.

The allotment holders mostly consume the produce of their land, which accounts for the difficulty there is in estimating yields; this, however, is a condition of success in small holdings, for it secures for the grower the profits of carrier, middleman, and retailer, which are a charge on the produce he sells. Partly for this reason, and partly because the plots are very carefully cultivated, the gross yields of Port Sunlight land compare very favourably with those of neighbouring farms. I am aware that it is not quite fair to contrast a hundred-acre farm with an allotment of a sixteenth of an acre when the former grows mainly wheat or grass and the latter vegetables, but it is possible to compare the Port Sunlight vegetable allotment with neighbouring swede or potato land. It is extremely difficult to obtain figures as to the

COTTAGES. [*To face p.* 102.

productivity of land, for farmers naturally conceal them (in those years when they are not being "ruined") for fear of seeing rents rise. Yet I was informed by land agents controlling some 3000 acres in the neighbourhood of Birkenhead that agricultural rents varied between 35*s.* and 50*s.* per acre, that they sometimes fell to 30*s.* an acre and that £2 was a very fair average; the figure of £2 net for Port Sunlight allotments is therefore evidence that the splitting up of farms may be to the landlord's advantage.* The tenant may, however, benefit to a still greater extent. Gross yields in Cheshire average £6 to £7 for good land; a few fields have produced £10 per acre under potatoes, but those instances are unfortunately rare: thus, it appears that, as the vegetable allotments at Port Sunlight produce on an average £4 to £5 for a sixteenth of an acre, or £60 to £80 per acre, the Port Sunlight average is quite seven times higher than one of the local records for productivity. This is not an unusual case, for in many parts of the country we find small holdings producing anything between three and twelve times as much as the surrounding land, but it is interesting to note it in view of the hostility manifested in various quarters by great landowners to the Small Holdings and Allotments Act (1907).

In addition to the allotments an interesting development of natural education is the "Children's Gardens" scheme. About a hundred small plots have been taken up by Port Sunlight boys and girls, and they are encouraged by a skilled instructor

* For encouragement to allotment holders, see Horticultural Society (Chapter VII.).

to take an interest in agricultural work. In addition, they are supplied with seeds at cost price and further helped by having their land dug. I would say, in this connection, that there appears to be a good deal of scope at Port Sunlight for increased facilities; at present the men purchase their seeds, tools, manure, etc., either from outsiders or from the store. If the store could keep all necessary articles in stock the arrangement might be fairly satisfactory, even if inferior to a special agricultural co-operative society, but owing to lack of space it cannot do so and profits go to outsiders. Since profits, though small, can actually be made out of such restricted areas it appears important to further at once the progress of a movement which has already rescued Irish dairy farming, placed Danish and Belgian agriculture on a pinnacle and shown us nearer at home—at Bewdley, at Framlingham, at Catshill, etc.—that mutual help and confidence can restore prosperity to the English country-side.

COTTAGES.

[*To face p.* 104.

CHAPTER VI

THE VILLAGE INSTITUTIONS (PUBLIC)

THE reader will have gathered from the preceding chapters that at Port Sunlight the conditions of life are likely to be agreeable, as agreeable at least as they can be made by work under the best of conditions, and housing both adequate and æsthetic. The joy of life is, however, bound up rather with the superfluous than with the necessary, so that Arcadia, ventilated and drained on the most scientific principles, would fall short of Utopia if the flowers of intellect and amity did not flourish within its pleasance. It is true that the essential charms of Port Sunlight are found by the fireside, and that life there is pre-eminently a story of the peaceful pleasures of home; it is, however, also true that without something to link together the inhabitants much of the object of the founder would have been missed.

Without its institutions Port Sunlight would not stand out so markedly as it does from among industrial villages; it could still boast of fine Works and good cottages, but it could not claim to have influenced directly the social habits of the people. To teach sobriety, cleanliness, and respect for the Law, something more is wanted than a good cottage.

For many men and women, especially if they are not so overworked as to desire no more than rest, the pleasures of the home do not suffice. If the people are to be rescued from drunkenness and immorality, the Good must fight the Evil with its own weapons and beat it at its own game. Why should the devil have all the good tunes? asked General Booth, and in the answer to that question we find the keynote of a social policy. The Church and the Chapel can and do achieve great work, but beyond their reach there lies an immense mass of our people by whose ears spiritual appeals remain unheard. To the low-class music hall we must oppose the theatre; to the drinking den we must oppose the ballroom, the concert hall, and the lecture room. It is only by giving pleasure for pleasure, and good measure of it, that we can hope to regain the ground lost by the beautiful and the pure.

Apart from such theoretical considerations it must be obvious that Port Sunlight could not hope to be a success unless the people had many opportunities of occupying their minds with sports and pastimes; it would be false to its educational principle if it only sought to make them comfortable, if it did not encourage them to develop their faculties and live to the full. Indeed, I am not sure that a population among whom an abnormal standard of comfort prevailed—abnormal that is in regard to its anterior conditions—without its intellectual standards rising at the same time, would not deteriorate and end like Stevenson's married man, by being so comfortable and happy as to begin to prefer comfort and happiness to everything else on earth. For that reason, particularly in a community which, like Port Sunlight, is neither rural nor urban, and has no great natural resources in the neighbourhood, it has been necessary to develop local organizations capable of ministering both to the needs and the pleasures of the people.

'It has been said that Port Sunlight is neither rural nor urban; it is not urban as we understand the term, for it is not a conglomeration of houses, fine in some parts, mean in others, dotted here and there with frigid public institutions, and rich mainly in those places where gross pleasures may be bought cheap. It must needs, therefore, rely upon itself for its pleasures, for it cannot go far afield in search of them. On the other hand, Port Sunlight is not rural, in so far as a village is rural, for it is too large, too active, and too young a community. Yet, as it has certain characteristics both of the village and of the town, it has to fear the perils of both, and the worst of these is boredom with the evils born of it, the idleness that drives the town worker into the public-house, the farm labourer into the city slum. How Port Sunlight is coping with these dangers by means both public and private will be realized from the following sketch of the institutions at work within the confines of the Village.

The public institutions comprise buildings and organizations such as are found in every community; the private institutions, controlled more directly by those who benefit by them, partake mainly of the nature of societies. The former minister to the intellectual development, and to the collective needs, of the people, the latter to their social pleasures; of the first class are the church, the public-house, the hospital, etc.; of the second class the various societies that have been formed for mutual entertainment and intercourse. It will be seen that it is difficult in classifying to avoid overlapping, for such institutions as the Auditorium and the Collegium might as well be placed in the second as in the first class, but there is the question of control. In the first class, therefore, we find those institutions which are more directly connected with and controlled by the Company, viz. the Auditorium, the Collegium, Bridge Inn, the Library and Museum, and the Hospital. In the second class are the Church and Sunday schools, athletic, literary, scientific, provident, and philanthropic societies (conducted as a rule exclusively by the employees), and the shops.

Both classes of institutions serve to link the people together, to promote friendliness and sociability, to make, briefly, life worth living as a life. They differ in so far as the first class comprises all the public buildings, but the objects of the two are fundamentally alike, so that it is possible to group them all under a common heading. Most of these institutions are, however, characteristic, so a short description of some of them will be interesting.

CHRIST CHURCH.—In the front rank of Port Sunlight institutions we find the church. In a community of some 3600 persons, where it is likely that a dozen denominations are represented, this might well have been a vexed question, and it is mainly because there is no religious trouble at Port Sunlight that it is important to go into the matter. For some unknown reason there have never been any religious difficulties at Port Sunlight, even in the very early

CHRIST CHURCH.

[*To face p.* 108.

days when services were held in Gladstone Hall and in the schools; a spirit of friendliness and tolerance appeared to reign, and peace has never been broken to this day. This spirit seems to have survived even the construction of a Congregational church, which bears eloquent witness to the good feeling that prevails. In the early days undenominational services were attended by persons professing various creeds, and the first congregations of the Church numbered among them about equal proportions of Churchmen and Nonconformists. This has continued to this day. A Roman Catholic chapel stands on the outskirts of the Village. The Wesleyans have also a place of worship; many of them still attend occasionally at Christ Church. There is a small Church of England chapel on the estate, and many more on the outskirts, Wesleyan and Presbyterian chapels being also fairly numerous. It will thus be seen from the foregoing that the Port Sunlighter is not placed in the predicament of having to accept local facilities or be deprived of religious teaching: his choice is entirely free. Christ Church being now Congregational, the building itself is vested in the Congregational Union, so as to prevent its ever falling into the hands of any other denomination; the minister must of course be approved by that body and appointed by Church members. The service book in use was compiled by a committee of 14, elected by ballot among the male worshippers; singularly enough, 7 out of the first 14 representatives belonged to the Church of England, as a result of which the form of service is to this day very largely based on the services of the Established Church. The Church now draws its resources from the seat-holders, each of whom pays as much as he thinks fit; as yet there is no endowment, which is perhaps as well, as every member is thus impelled to take a personal interest in the Church; there are, of course, some free seats in one of the transepts. Christ Church accommodates 600 worshippers, and at a pinch 800, or even 900. Before dismissing the subject it should be mentioned that the congregation of Christ Church includes, in addition to members of the Anglican and the various Nonconformist Churches, a few Unitarians and some Agnostics; during the seven years of the late minister's pastorate there was no sign of a dispute. This is remarkable, for religious feeling runs so high in the district that parliamentary elections are sometimes to a great extent fought on dogmatic issues * and that many advertisements for servants in the neighbourhood stipulate that applicants must profess a given religion!

Apart from its value as a spiritual agent, Christ Church is an object of beauty, for it is one of the most perfectly designed modern churches that have been erected in England. In style it is early perpendicular, pure and somewhat austere in its lines, rich in a simplicity relieved by the choice of the material out of which it is built: red sandstone, perfectly smooth, warm and grateful to the eye. Set in the midst of green fields and bounded by deep grass-grown dells, the squat tower of Christ Church gives to the traveller as pleasant a greeting as he would receive from the grave and ivy-clad church of a lonely village.

THE AUDITORIUM.—Leaving aside religion and religious matters, we find among the public buildings

* Kirkdale division of Liverpool, 1908.

THE AUDITORIUM. [*To face p.* 110.

an institution of some originality, the Auditorium, which was once an open-air theatre. Originally it was planned to occupy the slopes of one of the dells, round which an arena was built, rising in tiers round a stage which was to occupy the greater part of one end. This was a fascinating scheme, and it suggested great possibilities of education and refinement for the people; it pointed above all to the rescue of the stage from the vulgarity and the puerility into which it is too often plunged. Unfortunately the English climate is no respecter of institutions, so that the example of Rome and Nimes was reluctantly abandoned, and in 1906 the Auditorium was roofed in. Diverted from its original objects, however, the Auditorium is a very fine hall, the floor space of which alone is about 80 feet long by 40 broad. At present it is a theatre and dancing hall with a parquet floor. The hall easily accommodates 250 couples; when it is desired to convert it into a concert room or a theatre chairs can be put in, which brings the total seating capacity to 2500 persons. There is no rake, but the stage at the end is raised, and there is a good view of it from every part of the hall; in front of the stage is a sunken orchestra as in an ordinary theatre. The roof is mainly glass and provided with broad slides, so that ventilation is perfect; in addition there are large windows all along the upper part, and provision is made for pumping air, cooled or warmed according to the season, by means of electric fans. There are five exits; all the doors open outwards. Behind and above the stage are a well-fitted green room and dressing-rooms for the actors of both sexes. Below the stage is a large store of scenery, most of which reproduces Village streets; this is used by travelling companies.

It will be seen from the foregoing that the Auditorium leaves little to be desired as a hall for entertainments, either as regards size or facilities; it is difficult to convey an idea of the beauty of its design or to understand its appeal until one has seen it filled with dancers. The balls are the great nights for the Auditorium; travelling theatrical companies come from time to time, but less often than they did at the inception, for they are not extensively patronized by the villagers. The hall is decidedly large, expensive to light and to warm; it is used occasionally for the purpose, also for concerts and political meetings, but its principal use is for dances. Some of these are arranged by the employees themselves, but the largest are given by the Company. During the winter weekly dances are planned in such a manner that every girl employed at the Works is invited twice. Girls over eighteen may submit the names of men to the social department, which issues invitations to them unless there be reasons that militate against them. I do not know how often the choice of the girls is vetoed, but I understand that the veto is unusual. At any rate, the present social secretary is certainly well fitted to be a liberal and tactful discriminator. Besides, he is not the sole authority; these dances are controlled by a committee, half of whose members are foremen and forewomen and half employees; thus private grievances are not likely to influence the arrangements for the dances, which are exceedingly popular and invariably crowded. Girls under eighteen are provided with partners by the Company. The friendliness and order

THE PARSONAGE, ETC. [*To face p.* 112.

that prevails in them is a feature of Port Sunlight, and is commented on more fully in the chapter dealing with the spirit that reigns in the Village.

THE COLLEGIUM.—In many respects the Collegium (or Girls' Institute, as it was formerly called) is more suitable for general purposes than is the Auditorium. It is much smaller, and only comprises the upper floor of the stores and the adjacent block. It is really a very large room with a white wainscoting and light green paper, a pleasant relief being produced by heavy oak beams; the walls are covered with pictures, and the general effect completed by a floor of polished boards. Here again the visitor is struck by the large French windows, which practically cut out the walls at either end and flood the room with light and air.

At one end is a good platform large enough for several speakers, so that the building can be used for small meetings and lectures; the Mutual Improvement Society, among others, meets there regularly about once a week. Classes and drills (mainly of the Boys' Brigade) take place there, and also small dances, so that the Collegium fills a rather important *role* in the Port Sunlight scheme; during the winter months it is engaged practically every night. The room is large enough to seat two hundred, or to accommodate fifty couples with ease; dances are organized there about once a month by the various clubs, the cost being about 3*s.* 6*d.* per couple. These dances are remarkably bright and successful; the girls are in high dresses, but a number of the men wear evening dress.

On the whole the Collegium is more convenient than the Auditorium, though it does not serve so many purposes; the Auditorium could be spared, but the

Collegium is practically a necessity. Probably a slightly larger hall, say half the size of the Auditorium, would also be useful, for Hulme Hall is rather inconvenient, owing to the necessity of shifting tables and chairs.

BRIDGE INN.—By this time the reader will have realized that the resources of the one institution most in request in English villages are not overtaxed: I mean the public-house. It is unfortunately too true that the poor opportunities of relaxation enjoyed by town workers are almost entirely absent in the country, where the labourer in search of society is absolutely driven to the local inn. In Port Sunlight, village though it may be, facilities for amusement are so numerous that a single licence has been found sufficient. This is interesting in the light of recent developments in licensing reform; there never was any serious opposition to the scale laid down by Mr. Asquith when introducing the Licensing Bill in 1908, and it is interesting to compare its standard with that which prevails at Port Sunlight. Here we find a community of some 3600 persons settled on an area of about 132 acres, *i.e.* about 27 persons per acre; under Mr. Asquith's scheme Port Sunlight would be placed in Class C of the schedule (26 to 50 persons per acre), and would then be entitled to one on-licence for every 600 persons, or six licences altogether. In view of this fact, it is interesting to note that Port Sunlight seems adequately provided for by one-sixth of the licensed house accommodation allowed even on a reduced scale. We must, of course, not lose sight of the fact that there are a good many licensed houses in the neighbourhood, but a visit to Bridge Inn is

BRIDGE INN.

[*To face p.* 114.

convincing proof that the people of the Village do not frequent it.

If Bridge Inn is not a haunt of the villagers it is certainly not because it is not pleasant; it is not too much to say that it is the prettiest and most comfortable building in the Village. Moreover, it combines all the attractions of a first-class inn with low prices; this is important from the point of view of temperance, for it would not be good to think that the deserted condition of the inn (in the evening), to which I can bear full witness, is caused by high prices which only drive men into neighbouring, lower-class houses. Bridge Inn, as its name indicates, is situated at one end of the bridge that crosses the deepest dell on the east. It consists of a central portion with two projecting wings; it is built of grey stone, and has a fanciful pointed roof, but the greatest of its charms lies in the fact that the courtyard formed by the wings is overlooked from the first floor by a wooden gallery running entirely round the yard in the style dear to Mr. Pickwick. Bridge Inn, though fitted with a bar and a smoking-room, is really a restaurant; one large room is devoted to a *table d'hôte*, and is mainly used by tourists, whilst another in the same wing is used as a cheap dining-room by some of the Factory workers and by employees of outside firms, such as carters, etc. About 200 men on an average are served every day in this room; the prices are low and accessible to the artisan: hot-pot, 3*d.*; joint and vegetables, 6*d.*; vegetables, tea, or coffee, 1*d.* This institution is a useful accessory to Gladstone Hall, and goes some little way towards fulfilling the catering requirement I indicated with reference to it.

Bridge Inn was conducted as a temperance house from October, 1900, to February, 1903. Little by little, however, the feeling grew in the Village that it should have a licence, and in July, 1902, a meeting was held to discuss the matter; some 300 villagers were present, and after some controversy a vote was taken, which resulted in 207 voting in favour of a licence and 70 against it. Mr. Lever had, however, stipulated a three-fourths majority, as he had serious misgivings as to the advisability of introducing licensed premises into the Port Sunlight scheme; it was therefore decided to submit the proposal to the test of the referendum, every adult male and female resident in the Village being given a vote. The campaign was rather too short, only two days, so that the temperance organizations did not have time to oppose the proposal; it was accordingly carried by 472 votes against 120. I mention this in detail because it embodies the principle of local option. The licence was accordingly granted to the Liverpool and District Trust Company, Limited, who began operations in May, 1903. It is by now certain that there has never been any reason to regret its establishment; indeed, that Bridge Inn has improved local conditions, for it attracted in the early days those who formerly left the Village to drink, so much so that they have almost lost the public-house habit. The sobriety of the people is remarkable; I passed several "Saturday nights" in the Village without seeing a single drunken man: in how many industrial communities could one do the same?

For various reasons the Trust public-house was not successful, although many of these houses are well supported in other districts. This was in a sense

BRIDGE INN.

[*To face p.* 116.

unfortunate, not so much because the inn fell once more into the hands of individuals, for Port Sunlight is not a pirate community, as that it ceased to be under public control. Under the Trust *régime* two out of six managers were elected by the villagers and four nominated by the Company; nowadays the six managers are all nominated, and there is no public control; however, Bridge Inn is doing well under a salaried man, and it is certainly a condition of temperance that it should not be run at a loss. The inception period (beginning in September, 1905) being now over, it is expected that the inn will shortly begin to show a credit balance which will go to the relief of the Village account. The only criticism that can be levelled at the inn is that there are no billiards; comfortable as it is, particularly as regards the smoking-room, it still needs this addition to make it truly the poor man's club. It has a six days' licence, and closes at 11 P.M.

THE LIBRARY.—It will be seen further on that counter attractions to the charms of Bridge Inn are not wanting in Port Sunlight; one of them is the combined library and museum. These two institutions share a block of cottages, the remainder of which accommodates the Collegium, the Employees' Provident Society, and the post-office. The museum is large, made up of the upper parts of about six houses, and lit as usual by broad roof windows; it is rich in interesting exhibits, most of which have been given or lent by Mr. W. H. Lever. They comprise mainly old pewter and watches, old English china, armour, antique furniture, Egyptian curios, and *articles de vertu;* we must not forget the bugle that sounded the charge of the Light Brigade and, an obvious feature at Port Sunlight, a large chemical exhibition. Attached to the latter is a special reading and workroom where the apprentices may consult text books and study every evening after hours. The museum is much appreciated, but it suffers from lack of pictures; the educational value of the beautiful is, in the early stages, limited by its obviousness: thus a few prints after Rossetti or some of the old English masters would be very welcome.

The library is of course the more popular of the two institutions; it is very large and has two reading-rooms, one for men and the other for women. Its shelves are well filled, for it already has four thousand volumes, of which half are fiction, and it is still buying; no newspapers are found there, but eight or nine magazines are kept in the reading-rooms. So as to give the people some personal interest in the institution the rule has been established that they must become members; as the subscription is only 2*d.* per annum it is not extraordinary that they should number some seven hundred; this subscription includes the use of the lending library. I mentioned above that half the library consisted of fiction. This is perhaps unfortunate, though novels have an educational value for those who, failing novels, would read penny dreadfuls; but it is worth noting that about one-half of the members read exclusively serious books; these are mainly historical, scientific or artistic: such books as the "Life of Lord Randolph Churchill" or "Modern Egypt" are usually bought as soon as published. The library lends out about twenty-five thousand volumes every year. There is also a good reference library containing a number of technical works which must be

LIBRARY AND MUSEUM.

[*To face p.* 118.

useful to the artisans and apprentices. The only fault that can be found with both these institutions is one to which I shall again have to allude, viz. that they are closed on Sundays. It is obvious that the staff must have a day of rest, but the value of educational and social institutions is a good deal impaired by Sunday closing, when the very people who most need help are thrown on their own, and often scanty, resources; one wonders whether the enthusiasm that animates so many religious workers to sacrifice so much of their leisure could not be used in a body of "Sabbath Workers" whose self-imposed mission it would be to minister to the innocent pleasures of their fellows on the day of idleness, when, as the proverb says, the devil often finds so much work to do. Such a movement is well worth initiating even if it should fly in the face of prejudice.

THE COTTAGE HOSPITAL.—The last of the public institutions is the hospital, or rather cottage hospital as it is rightly called. It accommodates only fourteen patients, by means of twelve beds and two cots, but it is in miniature a perfect replica of our most modern urban hospitals; indeed, to describe it is to run the risk of praising it overmuch, so complete in every way are its arrangements and so intelligent is its planning. The building itself would have been graceful if the architect had not thought fit to run his chimneys up like smokestacks; on the whole, however, its light grey, rough-cast walls, casemented windows, and green shutters form a pretty picture. It is set on high ground and surrounded on every side by large open spaces, the football field and a well-wooded dell. It has a fairly large garden facing due south. The interior arrangements are spacious, I should say wastefully so, if space were not so cheap at Port Sunlight that all may enjoy the blessing of it. There are two wards, one for either sex, a surgery, waiting-room, a conservatory, a large staff room and a dining-room for the nurses, a special kitchen, nurses' rooms and doctor's quarters.

The Port Sunlight wards are in themselves the best of their kind; they are exceedingly spacious and not less than fifteen feet high; the windows might have been larger and the small panes done away with, for they accumulate dirt: that is my one adverse criticism. The floors are wood blocks and the walls are distempered, so that the entire surface can be drenched; indeed this passion for cleanliness is simply obtrusive: the floors of the corridors are tiled, the tables glass-topped; even the patients' lockers are washable; all floor and wall angles are rounded so that dust cannot collect. Ventilation is of course excellent; air is forced in after being either dried or moistened, warmed or cooled; all heating is done by steam. Everywhere are evidences of the love of comfort: the waiting-room is supplied with mahogany chairs; the baths (compulsory) are equal to those of a first-class hotel; the patients are provided with a conservatory facing south, where the women can sit and the men smoke. Provisions against fire are also complete, for hose and nozzles light enough to be used by women are supplied and the nurses are drilled every month.

The staff comprises the doctor (who lives on the premises and controls the ambulance corps), the matron, one staff nurse, and two nurses; there are

THE POST-OFFICE. [*To face p.* 120.

also three maids, another evidence of the esteem in which cleanliness is held. As a result cases are quickly disposed of, and it is not often that the hospital is full. Of course no charges are made. It may be remarked incidentally that such revelations of dirt as are frequent on the admission of patients to city institutions are not usual in Port Sunlight; I was informed at the hospital that, although the people are not as clean as the ubiquitous bathroom should make them, their standard is far superior to that attained by London, Manchester, and other industrial centres, a welcome fact, but one which should be the normal result of the improved conditions of the workers.

Before passing on to the institutions that more directly concern the employees, mention should be made of the shops, because they (or the buildings that contain them) are the property of the Company. There are not many shops at Port Sunlight, as the Employees' Provident Society (or co-operative society) caters for the immediate needs of the inhabitants; there are also various shops at Bebington and New Ferry. In the Village itself, in addition to the keepers of the store and post-office, there are only four tradesmen—a butcher, a hairdresser, a draper, and a newsagent. There is nothing to mention of special interest, except that the buildings are more sightly and the interiors cleaner than those which we usually find in villages and small towns.

CHAPTER VII

THE VILLAGE INSTITUTIONS (PRIVATE)

INTERESTING as the public buildings and larger institutions may be, the societies that are controlled solely by the men are perhaps of more importance, for in their development and prosperity we find the true evidences of intellectual health. It is beyond discussion that a community for which everything is done must deteriorate. So many institutions, among which those connected with the Works are the most important, are controlled by the Company, that it seems as if the Sunlighters must suffer. However, they have not done so: their social spirit is vigorous and their clubbable tendency is strong.

I need not dilate upon the subject in general, for the best evidence of this lies in the following list of societies and institutions organized and controlled by the employees (it is roughly classified) :—

Boys' Brigade.
Band of Hope.
Young People's Temperance League.
Anti-Cigarette League.
National British Women's Temperance Association.
Bellringers.
Church Choir.

THE GYMNASIUM.

[*To face p.* 122.

Philharmonic Society.
Orchestral Society.
Silver Prize Band.
International Bible Reading Association.
Mutual Improvement Society.
Scientific and Literary Society.
Men's Social and Bowling Club.
Horticultural Society.
Chess Club.
Football Clubs.
Gymnastic Club.
Swimming Club.
Rifle Club.
Tennis Club.
Cycling Club.
Maternal Aid Society.
Women's Guild.
Sick, Medical, and Funeral Aid Society.
St. John's Ambulance Brigade Division.
Clerks' Dining Club.
Employees' Provident Society.

This list does not include various school institutions and those connected with the Works; apart from them, therefore, the people of Port Sunlight find time to run twenty-eight institutions, which is certainly a respectable number. Of the social spirit, which is strong, more is said in another chapter; here we need not examine in detail all the various societies, but we must give particulars of a few of the more important or successful ones.

THE GYMNASIUM.—Among the athletic societies the gymnasium is certainly the most interesting. The building itself is very large, for it contains three halls, the smallest of which is forty feet long; the largest can easily accommodate a hundred performers when display drills are given. Each hall is provided with full sets of apparatus in duplicate and in triplicate; the object of this is to allow of boys, girls, and men being trained at the same time. The gymnasium is open to all (every night during the week) on payment of a yearly subscription of 3*s.* 6*d.* for men, and 2*s.* for girls and boys; non-residents and non-employees may join at a rate increased by 1*s.* 6*d.* This club is very successful, for it has a membership of over two hundred, of which ninety are girls; its proficiency is above the ordinary, for I was informed that it had beaten Liverpool, the Balfour Institute, St. Saviour's, Everton, etc. I can well believe it after seeing the zest which both sexes display at the practices. The men are dressed, as a rule, in white vests and running shorts, the girls in smart blue and red serge costumes; the musical drills executed by massed groups are bewildering in their intricacy.

The gymnasium also runs a basket-ball section, which is so popular that there are no less than eight teams. Its future is assured, for an instructor is provided for the boys and girls; I would mention here that attendance is not compulsory for the children. It is, of course, impossible to force them to come to the gymnasium so long as physical training is not part of the school curriculum, but a system of premiums, free membership, and prizes would certainly influence the youth of Port Sunlight for their greater benefit.

THE SWIMMING CLUB.—Another interesting institution is the swimming club. The bath itself is well worthy of notice, for it enjoys the unusual distinction

THE OPEN-AIR BATH.

[*To face p.* 124.

of being an open-air bath. This, though it has its disadvantages in a cold country, is certainly a step in the right direction, for none will deny that such vigorous exercise as swimming increases in value if it is taken in the open air. The Port Sunlight bath is a very good one, for it is some hundred feet long by seventy-five broad; in shape, it is a rough oval; in depth it varies between three feet three inches and seven feet three inches; the water can be warmed as desired. Originally it was built for the sole use of the inhabitants of Port Sunlight, but it has since then been opened to outsiders joining the swimming club. In connection with the open-air bath is the strong Swimming and Life Saving Society, which has three hundred and fifty members, and is represented in the Northern Counties Association; residents and employees are admitted at a charge of 1*s.* per annum, non-residents at 2*s.*, children at half fees. All the members may be trained not only in swimming but in life-saving and water-polo. This game is much in favour, and the Port Sunlight team won last year no less than eight out of eleven contested matches.

THE CLUB.—While athletics are at a premium in Port Sunlight, educational and social institutions are equally well supported by the older men. The most important of these is probably the men's social and bowling club, better known in the Village as "The Club." This is a fairly large building in the early English style, standing in its own grounds, and provided with a bowling-green and a quoiting-field; it takes up altogether about an acre and a-half. The ground floor is occupied by the reading-room, where some half-dozen dailies and twenty or thirty weeklies are kept. I noted with some pleasure that the selection was so thoroughly catholic that *The Freethinker* rubbed shoulders with *The Christian World.* In this room cards and chess may be played, but not for money. Upstairs there is a billiard-room with tables large enough for a comfortable lounge. Full membership is open to residents and employees for 5*s.* per annum, or membership of either the reading-room, the bowling-green, or the chess room for 2*s.* 6*d.*; there are about one hundred and twenty members. This institution is entirely self-supporting; but it pays no rent for the use of the grounds or building, defrays the cost of lighting, heating, newspapers, etc., and engages its own caretaker; in spite of its small budget it makes ends meet. These are important facts, for it is not desirable that clubs should depend on an employer; at present the club pays its way fully. The club is open daily for about seven hours (Saturdays ten and a half), but it is closed on Sundays; no alcoholics are sold, but only temperance drinks.

On the whole the club is well worthy of notice as well for its many good points as for its serious failings. On the other hand, it is remarkable for its orderliness; for the way in which fifty or sixty men at a time seem to find there recreation without brawls or evil language; for the democratic spirit that reigns in it, and unites in their games foremen and labourers of all grades. This, in fact, is for the visitor the principal attraction of the club, for it shows that men in different positions can mix successfully, and be drawn together for their mutual benefit. On the other hand, the club shows two serious defects, and it is likely that if they were corrected the membership would go up by leaps and

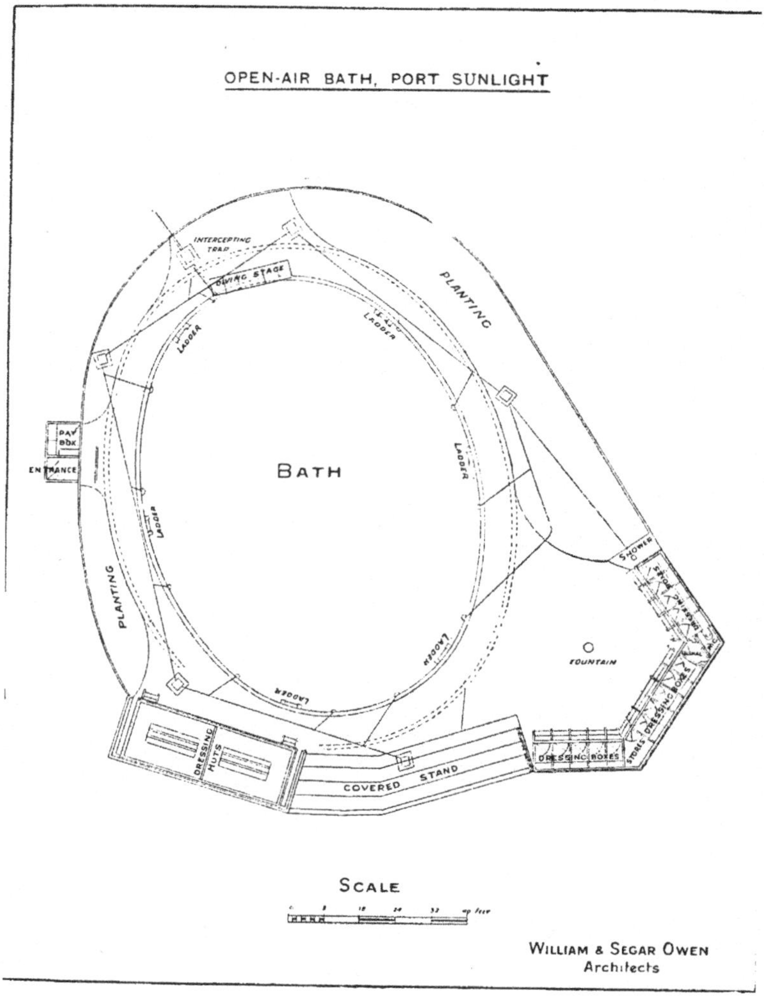
OPEN-AIR BATH, PORT SUNLIGHT
INTERCEPTING TRAP
DIVING STAGE
PLANTING
LADDER
LADDER
PAY BOX
ENTRANCE
BATH
LADDER
LADDER
PLANTING
SHOWER
DRESSING BOXES
FOUNTAIN
LADDER
LADDER
DRESSING HUTS
COVERED STAND
DRESSING BOXES
STORES
DRESSING BOXES
SCALE
WILLIAM & SEGAR OWEN
Architects

[*To face p.* 126.

bounds; the one is Sunday closing, and the other temperance. I do not plead against Sunday closing in general, but it is indisputable that certain institutions and trades must be exempted, and that, in those cases, we must substitute "one day's rest in seven" for "the seventh day." The principal value of a club lies in the fact that it is a home ever open to the member who is away from his dwelling, or in want of a change of scene; to give him an opportunity of amusement in the evening is well, but to leave on his hands the one day that is entirely his, a day which may be wet, lonely, or dull, that is bad, for the essential functions of a club are stultified. Whether Sunday opening can be provided for by voluntary effort or by extra help I do not pretend to say, but it seems that a club numbering one hundred and twenty members could arrange for one member to replace the caretaker every Sunday, when each member would, by means of the sacrifice of one Sunday in about two years, secure for himself the freedom of the club for the other one hundred odd Sundays.

The other weakness of the club is the fact that no alcoholic liquor is supplied; this is not a pleasant remark for a temperance worker to have to make, but no one can be blind to the fact that people will have intoxicants, and that they will go in great numbers where these are sold. The question then arises: are we to let the public-house entice away to extravagance and debauchery men whom we might have retained by allowing them reasonable facilities? It is quite true that many public-houses are orderly, and that many clubs are drinking hells, but surely it is not beyond the power of a *disinterested* institution to enforce moderation upon its members by expelling any man who abused his liberty. It is not good to allow the Puritan spirit, which has made England great, but has also made it in some respects hard and narrow, to interfere with the enjoyment of the ordinary good things of life and, worse still, to drive to vicious pleasures those whom it desired to cure by unsympathetic force, and in spite of themselves. I speak strongly in this case, but it is hard to see an institution rich in so many possibilities hampered and hindered in its usefulness by being deprived of the common privileges of freedom.

THE MUTUAL IMPROVEMENT SOCIETY.—An institution deserving of all praise, on the other hand, is the Mutual Improvement Society, the aim of which is "to promote a truly fraternal spirit among the residents and employees of Port Sunlight." The society pursues this object by means of a course of lectures from October to March, broken by socials, evenings with the poets, etc. It is accessible at the low rate of 1*s.* per annum, and has about one hundred and fifty members. It is self-supporting but for the occasional loan of a hall; it defrays the cost of lighting and heating and the expenses of lecturers. The lectures deal with varied subjects and questions of the day, such as travels, scientific subjects, etc. For instance, in the 1907–8 calendar I note amongst others lectures on Japan, the Prevention of Consumption, Physical Training, Bournville, Socialism, etc. Most of these lectures are given by specialists, and may be discussed; these evenings are well attended and are held at the Collegium.

SCIENCE, MUSIC, AND LITERATURE.—Somewhat

THE CLUB.

[To face p. 128.

similar in their objects are the Scientific and Literary Society, the Philharmonic Society, and the Orchestral Society, for they also aim at grouping the people for educational and social purposes. The Scientific and Literary Society attempts to foster by means of lectures, debates, and the reading of papers an interest in the subjects indicated by its name; among its latest lectures are such matters as "Sound waves," "The X rays," "George Eliot," "The Holy Wells of Cornwall," etc. The society also makes a strong point of nature study, particularly botany, and promotes trips into the neighbouring country. It is entirely self-governed and self-supporting, the only help it receives being the loan of a hall, which it must light and warm; though its subscription is low (men *2s.*, women *1s.*, per annum) it manages to make ends meet; its membership is about eighty, and consists mainly of the analysts of the Works, foremen, clerks, and their wives.

The two musical societies are under the leadership but not under the control of the musical director. He is an official of the Company, and his existence is a striking token of the interest that the authorities take in the encouragement of the arts. The musical director is organist at the church, acts as conductor to the Philharmonic Society and the Orchestral Society, and advises both generally on programmes, etc. Both societies are flourishing; the Philharmonic admits none but employees and their families, and has seventy members. Its work is entirely choral, and consists in performances of glees, oratorios, etc. Though the subscription is only *2s. 6d.* a year for men and *2s.* for women, the society manages to light and heat its hall, supply music free to members, and pay an orchestra when required. It clears its deficits by giving three large concerts every season, when it hires the Auditorium, to which the public are admitted at prices varying between 1*s.* and 1*d.* The Orchestral Society is also primarily an employees' society, but has to admit a few outsiders so as to secure all the necessary instrumentalists; it has about thirty members and is also entirely self-supporting: it even pays the caretaker of the schools a small fee whenever it holds a practice. The Silver Prize Band is distinct from these societies and has been successful in various northern competitions.

THE HORTICULTURAL SOCIETY.—The last of the educational societies for which I can find space is the Horticultural Society. This organization (which is entirely controlled by employees) has as a primary object the encouragement of the allotment holders by means of a yearly flower and vegetable show. It is open to all allotment holders and employees at a subscription of 1*s.* per annum; prizes varying between 1*s.* and 12*s.* 6*d.* are given for the best kept allotments and the finest selection of vegetables; in addition some prizes and cups are given by firms of seedsmen, a special prize of two tons of manure being well worth winning. A good feature is the show for children's gardens, for which prizes varying from 2*s.* to 7*s.* 6*d.* are put up. Generally speaking, Port Sunlight produce eclipses that of the neighbourhood, as is natural enough on small allotments,* and the show is quite one of the events of the year. The society has over 100 members, and is certainly doing very good work, but it might well do more. Where the

* See Chapter V.

THE CLUB.

THE CLUB: BILLIARD ROOM.

[*To face p.* 130.

holdings are so small and their number so large as in Port Sunlight, there is a crying need for more extensive facilities; the store sells tools but it does nothing more: the allotment holders must buy their seeds and manures elsewhere and in small parcels, so that they pay far too high rates. It is surprising that they have not organized a small purchasing society, which could also arrange for the distribution and exchange of produce. The Horticultural Society might easily take over this work, as it would require but little capital, and its value to the community would thereby be considerably increased. It is obvious that the people would (1) save a great deal by buying wholesale; (2) save freight by grouping in truck loads; (3) most important of all, secure a constant supply of fresh manures.

EMPLOYEES' PROVIDENT SOCIETY STORE.—A direct evidence of the value of co-operation at Port Sunlight is given by the prosperity of the Employees' Provident Society, better known as "The Store." This is quite an important feature of Port Sunlight, in fact the only important shop, and it has almost a monopoly of trade in the Village. It is not necessary to praise the co-operative system, particularly when applied to distribution: the fact that co-operative dealings exceed a hundred million pounds per annum in the United Kingdom bears eloquent enough witness to the merits of the method. The Port Sunlight society is purely an employees' society, controlled and financed entirely by them; it has no connection with the Company except in so far as it pays a commercial rent to the Village account. Its control is very minutely provided for by means of rules which are substantially the same as those issued by the Co-operative Union, Ltd.; the store is a member of this federation, as also of the English Wholesale Co-operative Society. It is not worth while, therefore, to reproduce these rules *in extenso*, but some points are worth quoting. Every member must hold shares to the value of at least £2; this is rather a large amount, but the rules allow of their being paid up at the rate of 3*d*. a week, with a fine of 1*s*. per quarter if payments fall into arrears; on the other hand, no member of the society may invest in it more than £200. Of course no dividends are paid out to any member until his shares are fully paid up, but provision is made for cases of distress. The society offers good opportunities for the investment of small sums by issuing withdrawable shares or accepting small loans at 5 to 6 per cent. interest; this rate appears high, but it is not unduly so, since the trading profits of the society vary between 7½ and 12 per cent., which leaves a fair margin of profit.

The democratic character of the society is preserved by the rule that every member shall have one vote irrespective of his shareholding. This essential feature of co-operation should not be lost sight of: I do not propose to deliver an assault on joint-stockism, but this recognition that from a relative point of view the interest of the rich and the poor are equal is at the root of the great progress of co-operation in this country. The employees of the store need not be members; this is the only fault I have to find with the society. It is not what Holyoake would have called a "dark" store, for the rules state that "the employees shall divide among them not less than

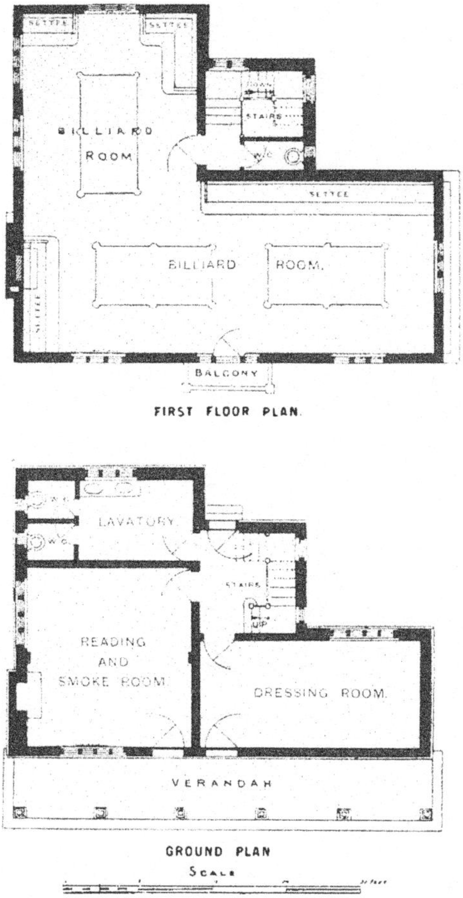

MEN'S SOCIAL CLUB, PORT SUNLIGHT

GRAYSON & OULD Architects

[*To face p.* 132.

a farthing in the pound on gross sales, or halfpenny in the pound on net profits," but their share is too small to give them much interest in the society; in fact, for last quarter they only divided £10 (in addition to their wages), and benefited to the extent of £5 11*s.* 6*d.* by a pleasure trip. This is not enough; they should have special facilities for constituting a small capital by means of an increased percentage on sales, even if their wages had to be reduced, by assimilating their labour to purchases, etc., by any method to be agreed upon, and of these there is no lack, that will give them a definite interest in the fortunes of the store.

There is no doubt, however, that the store is very successful, so successful in fact that I reproduce below the record of its career.

The last line of figures bears only upon half a year, and cannot be readily compared with the preceding ones, even if we multiply them by two, for quarters vary. It is, however, obvious that the society has expanded regularly; at the present time it has 556 members in 720 houses, a very high proportion even in the few cases where there are several members in one house. The average distribution of two shillings in the pound is about equal to that of distributive societies in Great Britain. The store occupies a fairly large floor space, of which, however, it has none too much, as it does most of the grocery trade of the Village; it also sells drapery, boots, ready-made clothing, coal, confectionery, etc., and even runs a bakery and a refreshment room.

The store is closely connected with the co-operative movement, for against sales amounting to about £16,000 per annum (equivalent to an outlay of £13,000 to £14,000), we find that about £7200 go to the

PROGRESS OF THE SOCIETY.

	No. of members.	Share capital.	Sales.	Net profit distributed.	Per annum average dividend.
		£ s. d.	£ s. d.	£ s. d.	s. d.
First year ending June 28, 1898 ..	173	378 10 11	6,020 5 1	463 14 0	1 6
Second ,, June 27, 1899 ..	210	509 5 8	5,951 12 8	426 11 9	1 8
Third ,, May 30, 1900 ..	311	743 8 5	7,676 19 3	584 7 1	1 8
Fourth ,, May 29, 1901 ..	386	1008 19 8	10,613 16 4	856 8 2	1 9
Fifth ,, May 28, 1902 ..	369	1031 16 1	10,930 7 9	1021 11 1	1 10
Sixth ,, May 27, 1903 ..	410	1397 2 10	13,581 18 10	1658 11 6	2 4
Seventh ,, May 25, 1904 ..	500	1924 7 3	15,536 18 3	1790 0 5	2 3
Eighth ,, June 7, 1905 ..	513	2230 0 3	15,753 18 2	1677 7 11	2 1
Ninth ,, June 6, 1906 ..	529	2487 14 8	15,027 15 4	1550 15 11	1 11¾
Tenth ,, June 5, 1907 ..	546	2454 12 5	15,816 9 5	1637 13 8	2 0
Eleventh ,, December 4, 1907 (half year)	556	2447 10 9	7,960 2 7	687 0 3	1 9

THE STORE. [*To face p.* 134.

Wholesale Co-operative Society and £600 to productive co-operative societies; this is certainly just as it should be. Lastly, as regards thrift, the average investment of each member is £4 8*s*. The store is managed on sound lines, and is not likely to come to grief, for the apportionment of the profits is defined by the rules. Plant is written down at so rapid a rate that it only stands in at present at about 35 per cent. of its cost, horses and conveyances at 25 per cent. There is also a reserve fund to be used for contingencies, equalization of dividends or *any charitable, philanthropic, or public object;* this is worthy of attention, for it at once lifts the society out of the purely mercantile rut into which it might so easily sink. The educational fund can be made to amount to 2½ per cent. of net profits, and can be used as directed by the general meetings; the development of the idea (which is not entirely novel) will be followed with interest.

SICK BENEFIT SOCIETY.—Another valuable instance of mutual help at Port Sunlight is the Sick, Funeral, and Medical Aid Society; it does not to any noticeable degree differ from ordinary benefit societies, yet the working of these is not so generally known as to make a few words about the Port Sunlight society superfluous. It has no connection with the Company except that as a matter of convenience the rules appoint Messrs. Lever Brothers trustees of the society's monies; this enables the society to do without a banking-account, and to earn interest. The Company will also, if requested to do so by a member, pay the subscriptions out of his or her weekly wages. Otherwise the society is run by the employees, who elect their own committee, appoint their own secretary and doctors, etc. The secretary is remunerated by means of a commission of 3 per cent. on subscriptions, fines and levies, equal to about £50 per annum; out of this he pays such clerical assistance as he may require.

There are some interesting provisions in the rules. There is one, for instance, that makes the post of a committee man effective, and ensures that the function will be taken seriously: non-attendance at meetings is, in default of good reasons, punished by fines of threepence for ordinary members, and sixpence for officers. I do not know what the effect of this rule has been, but it speaks well for the public spirit of the men that there are always candidates from every department for any of the vacant seats. Another onerous position is that of the "stewards," or "sick visitors," who are elected quarterly by the committee for the purpose of inquiring into the cases reported to the society, and of preventing fraud. These duties carry no salary, and their non- or ill-fulfilment renders the steward liable to expulsion from the society; this again speaks well for the public spirit of the members. Five pounds per annum are set aside to provide appliances for those who cannot afford them.

All employees between fourteen and forty-five, their wives and children are, after medical examination, admissible to the full benefits; above these ages they can be admitted if passed both by the doctor and the committee. This admission or retention on the books of the older men, most of whom are or will soon be pensioners, is in a sense a source of danger to the stability of the society; but it would be hard and unfair to deprive a man of benefits for which he was ready to pay because he was in receipt of a pension. Subscriptions are on three scales, according to age. Class A includes juniors (both sexes, under eighteen), Class B is for females over eighteen, and is open to males under twenty-one, Class C is for males not included in the other two classes. Subscriptions and benefits can best be seen from the following table:—

	WEEKLY		BENEFITS ON DEATH OF		
	Subscriptions.	Sick benefit.	Member.	Member's wife.	Member's child, under 14 years of age.
Class A	2*d.*	3*s.*	£3	—	—
„ B	3*d.*	5*s.*	£4	£3	£1
„ C	6*d.*	10*s.*	£8	£6	£2

This table at first sight does not seem very nicely adjusted, as Class A appears to be at a disadvantage, but it must be remembered that it only includes young persons under eighteen whose needs are greater and whose illnesses are frequent; moreover, the society must take into account the considerable help that is given by Messrs. Lever Brothers, who increase by 50 per cent. the subscriptions of all the females and those of the boys in Class A. This voluntary item is a large one and amounted in 1907 to almost £180, or 9 per cent. of the total receipts of the society.

The above benefits are granted for thirteen weeks, after which half benefit is paid for another thirteen weeks, and quarter benefit for such period as the committee may fix. A man may also secure medical aid and medicine for his wife at the rate of 1*d.* a week, and for every child under fourteen for an additional penny; he may secure medical aid only for his mother or wife's mother, if resident, at 1*d.* a week. All benefits are, of course, subject to certificates granted by one of the society's four doctors, and the serving out of medicine to the production of the card of membership.

The financial position of the society is particularly strong, and the contribution of Messrs. Lever Brothers is not needed to balance the accounts; indeed, this contribution in 1907 amounted to only a quarter of the realized surplus for the year; the sole object of the contribution is to encourage thrift among the younger and poorer sections of the employees; the fact that it is not paid on the contribution of Class C is counterbalanced by this class participating in the total surplus. The Port Sunlight society divides its surplus every year, so that it is a savings' bank as well as a provident fund; in 1907 every member of Class A received 4*s.* 8*d.*, of Class B 7*s.*, and of Class C 14*s.* The total benefit for the year (including doctors' fees) amounted to £1071; as the total membership was 1459 it is clear that undue use of their privileges is not common among the employees. I mentioned above that surpluses were divided. In 1907 the divisible surplus was £729 4*s.* 2*d.*, and a sum of £62 3*s.* 3*d.* was constituted into a reserve. This proceeding is not above criticism; it is true that the popularity of the society would be impaired if it attempted to form a strong reserve, and that its functions as a savings' bank would be interfered with, but it is clear that the position is not as stable as it should be. At present all is well with the society, and its members are mostly young and vigorous, but how will it fare within, say twenty years, when sick benefits and, still more, funeral benefits become heavy? We shall then see either the surpluses shrinking, and with them the popularity and the membership of the society, or levies will be necessary, in which case the results will be still worse. The only safe policy is to set aside every year a fixed proportion of the profits, say 10 per cent. of the surplus, until the society has at least 10*s*. per member in hand. To do this would cost the three classes only 5*d*., 8½*d*., and 1*s*. 3*d*. per head and per annum for about nine years, after which surpluses could be divided in full. Such a course would be slightly unfair to the present members, as they might leave the society, but they all have equal chances; besides, their position is somewhat similar to that of shareholders in a company which is constituting a reserve, for they may sell their shares, and yet they are not likely to find the amount of the reserve reflected by the price they obtain. At any rate, in so serious a question as the future of a benefit society doctrinaire justice must give way to the exigencies of sound finance.

WOMEN'S GUILD, AND MATERNAL AID SOCIETY. —Before leaving this already lengthy survey of Village institutions a few words should be said on two institutions, both partly philanthropic, the object of which is to lighten or brighten the lot of the women. One is the Women's Guild, the other the Maternal Aid Society. The Women's Guild is almost self-supporting, and has about one hundred members. Its objects are fellowship, and religious and social intercourse. Primarily it is intended to give women whose family duties prevent them from going to church an opportunity of spiritual refreshment, but various other aims are also attained. The mothers are allowed to bring their children and their sewing, which they cheerfully pursue while the minister expounds a short lesson. Then tea and refreshments are handed round whilst the secretary reads announcements, and here we find an interesting development. To encourage women's interest in the affairs of the people lectures are given from time to time on subjects that interest them particularly, such as temperance, housing, hygiene, Acts of Parliament affecting the child, etc. At a meeting at which I was present, for instance, an account of a temperance debate was read and a petition largely signed.

The Women's Guild is also a savings' bank; members pay in anything between 3*d.* and 1*s.* 6*d.* at any meeting, and on this they receive the large bonus of 2*d.* in the shilling, paid out of the proceeds of a jumble sale held every year; the goods (mainly clothing and groceries) are gifts from outsiders and are sold to the women at low rates. The proceeds suffice to pay expenses, bonuses, rent and lighting of room, etc., so that the society is only partly philanthropic. The guild also organizes picnics, and strives, in brief, to shed a little light upon lives which are but too often drab and cheerless.

The Maternal Aid Society does not differ greatly from similar associations formed in many parishes. It is philanthropic, but is based on self-help. Its object is to assist the wives of the less well paid employees by supplying them with a bag of linen for mother and baby, a portion of which is retained, as well as with some groceries. The bag is lent for one month. In addition the society pays for the doctor, the nurse and the washing; the total cost per bag is about 32*s.*, but the charge made to the mother is only 5*s.*; as this is insufficient, voluntary effort has to make up the deficit. The society does excellent work, particularly in large families, for the benefit society does not provide for confinements.

THE SOCIAL SECRETARY.—There are many minor points in the other societies worthy of mention, but their discussion would lead us to digress too far. The *rôle* of the social secretary is, however, so closely interwoven with the societies themselves that his position should be explained. The institution of a social secretary may be made to mean a great deal or very little; in some American factories his principal occupation is to stand between master and men, to state grievances and obtain redress, to intercede in favour of culprits, to organize leagues, societies, and sports, to work for the welfare of the men in every way that his ingenuity can suggest. At Port Sunlight his work is rather different, for he does not play the part either of advocate or peacemaker; the intimate contact that appears to exist between the head officials and the employees has reduced the necessity for this kind of intervention to a minimum. The social secretary of the Village is in charge of the welfare of the institutions; he arranges for them the use of halls, printing and advertising, provides lectures, entertainments, etc. He is a member of more than one committee, and is secretary to the Auditorium, the hospital, the mutual improvement society, and the club. He often receives and sometimes acts as a guide to visitors, and assists press-work. He is, in fact, rather secretary to the institutions than social secretary; as he controls all the public buildings and must always be ready to give every encouragement and aid to the societies his is by no means a sinecure. The successful social secretary must not only be a hard worker but a man of wide sympathy, having the interest of the people at heart, and a kindly understanding of that which is both good and pleasant in their eyes. In fact, it lies very much in his hands to make or to mar the social life of the Village, a great task and a great responsibility. In view of all that has been said in this chapter and in Chapter VI. the reader will gather that a very high tribute of praise is due to the present social secretary; I have certainly tried to do him justice in the preface.

A few institutions such as the Boy's Brigade, the Bible class, and the Sunday school offer features of interest, but they are of so special a nature that they have been incorporated into the chapter dealing with education, in connection with which, and with Chapter III., this account of Port Sunlight institutions should be read.

CHAPTER VIII

SOME RESULTS

IN social as in other schemes the proof of the pudding is in the eating. Thus no innovation is justifiable unless it can be shown that it has really been an improvement; this is perhaps a truism, but the world unfortunately seems to be divided into two camps, those who would pull down everything and those who would pull down nothing. I confess that my sympathies go out to the iconoclasts, not only because they are vigorous and idealistic, even though sometimes mistaken, but because there is always a presumption that an old law is a bad law, an old institution a bad institution. At any rate the onus of proof is with the ancient and presumably outworn system, not with the young if upstart theory. I do not suppose that this view is acceptable to everybody, but, after all, a view acceptable to everybody is usually good for nobody, for the merit of a scheme is measured by the numbers of its detractors.

The value of social schemes, however, is only thus measured at the inception; in later stages they must justify their existence by their results and by nothing else, for the practical social student will always prefer one small gain to ten valiant efforts. To what extent, therefore, may we ask ourselves, has Port Sunlight succeeded? To what degree has it modified the habits of the people? In what direction has it influenced their minds? I do not hesitate to say that the fields of social effort have seldom been tilled to greater advantage, and that the effects, both moral and material, of good housing and good general conditions are in many ways remarkable. Not only are we struck by the appearance of the Village, so much struck that, secure in the challenge and confident of victory, we can say to the incredulous: Go and see! but if we go further and observe more closely the habits of the people, we have it borne upon us that our own social system is sorely out of joint. That good conditions could have had such striking effects within twenty years is enough to make us bitterly conscious of the guilt of our town builders, of the faithless shepherds who neglect their flocks.

On the moral side, in no direction has Port Sunlight made its influence so strongly felt as in that of temperance. It is true that there is in the Village only one licensed house, and that the club sells no intoxicants; thus the temptations that assail the worker at every street corner in our cities of grime and gold are absent in the Village. There is, however, something more, for within a quarter of a mile of the boundaries of the Village there are altogether no fewer than thirteen public-houses, some far from dirty or uninviting. Opportunities for drunkenness are therefore present, I do not say to as great a degree as they would be in a great city, but not to so much less a degree as might explain the unusual sobriety of the people. For, indeed, what do we see at Bridge Inn but numbers of factory workers purchasing food and non-intoxicants—a few going so far as to take a single drink, but no more. Except at meal times the inn is deserted; the bar at which in other houses we are accustomed to see a small crowd is frequented only by visitors. Yet the inn is far from unattractive; everything possible has been done to turn it into a true "poor man's club"; the cosy smoking-room has been described in Chapter VI., and it might be expected that its comfortable padded seats would attract the men in shoals, and detain them for whole evenings at a time. The liquor is good and the prices are low, and yet, in the face of all inducements (or rather apparent inducements) the men do not come. For this there are only two explanations: the men have either gone elsewhere or found something better to do. The first explanation is natural enough when we consider that Bridge Inn lies in the middle of the Village, for the residents might not care to be seen in the bar; on the other hand, we must remember that there are in Port Sunlight one thousand seven hundred men and women over twenty-one, so that, if they frequented the public-houses in the neighbourhood, it would be noticeable. Yet visits to several of these houses give no reason to think that the people of Port Sunlight have resort to them to any great extent; one can generally recognize the inhabitant, if only by his healthy appearance, and I do not think that the neighbouring houses enjoy very much of his patronage. The second is thus the only alternative: the Sunlighter does not drink. The fact is that he does not need to drink. He has a comfortable home, and he is therefore more inclined to stay there than to go out to buy society at the cost of many drinks; I repeat that which cannot be said too often: a good home and drunken habits are almost incompatible, save in the case of natural vice. It is almost certain that drunkenness is a self-engendered habit, for men rarely begin by drinking to excess. In the first place, particularly when they are bachelors, they drink for the sake of conviviality—they increase their consumption of alcoholics because excitement decreases with satisfaction; if their homes are wretched the contrary state to the bachelor's loneliness has similar results. At Port Sunlight, where family feeling reigns supreme, the man is not driven out of his home by squalor, but prefers to dwell there in quietude and ease.

Whatever be the causes, and every social student will agree that good housing is the root cause, the fact remains that the drink bill of Port Sunlight is very low. I have no reliable statistics as to the workers' budgets, but it is on the face of it impossible that any family in the Village attains the fearful figure of *7s.* a week,* given by Dr. Dawson Burns and Sir Thomas Whittaker, which is the average expenditure on stimulants of working-class families. Indeed, it is likely that the Trust public-house failed because it attained its object too well, and that the present management would already have shared its fate if the inn had not been transformed into a catering establishment. The fact therefore remains, and it will be hard to disprove it, that one of the first effects of twenty years of good housing has been a deep and probably radical transformation of habits said to be hereditary, but due in reality to an apparently hopeless combination of evils:

* See also Messrs. Rowntree and Sherwell's calculations.

the evils have been fought and conquered, and drink, the cause and result of social questions, has at once been conquered with them. Anything more cheering and strengthening for those who are struggling with social problems than the state of things at Port Sunlight I can hardly conceive.

Cleanliness, next to godliness, is surely next to sobriety. A sidelight in Chapter VI., dealing with the revelations of the hospital, shows that the influence of the ubiquitous bathroom has made itself felt. I am aware that one of the charges commonly levelled at the working classes is that their standards of cleanliness are low; all I can say is that, given the conditions under which too large a section lives, it is surprising that their standard is as high as it is. The inhabitants of model dwellings and of the better class cottages are not badly off as regards facilities, for they have either common baths at their disposal, or enough space to perform their ablutions in private. But when we come to the tenement dwellers the position is very different. Many of the tenement houses in Whitechapel, Poplar, Islington, etc., were formerly good middle-class residences in Georgian or early Victorian days; little by little these districts have been deserted for the benefit of the suburbs, and the houses have been divided up into one- or two-roomed tenements. Naturally enough, as our fathers did not attach so much importance to this question of cleanliness as to provide bathrooms themselves, the owners of the decadent properties did not make good their omissions. Thus the tenement dweller, when he is fortunate, must often draw his water supply from a tap on the landing, sometimes from a pump in the back-yard. All I would ask the middle-class critic is whether his zeal would be stimulated by having, on a frosty morning, to fetch a bucket of cold water from the pump for the purpose of washing, possibly in the presence of the whole family?

The Sunlighter is free from these terrible disabilities, and a few days' intercourse with him is enough to show that he believes fervently in the gospel of soap and water both for himself and his house. I visited some of the smaller dwellings in the Village and was everywhere struck by the spotless condition of floors and walls, the neatness of the white curtains, the general well-scrubbed appearance of every household article. The secret was revealed to me by an artisan's wife who remembered but too well the "Scotland" division of Liverpool: "The houses are respectable, so we keep ourselves respectable." In that sentence is summed up the housing problem, with all that it means in terms of human suffering and of human potentialities. How far reaching the effects of the Port Sunlight scheme have been as regards temperance and cleanliness is obvious to all who care to observe: after a day they will be convinced; there are other directions, however, in which good housing has been at work, one of them being general morality.

It is too often thought that morality, "perceived obligation," is the exclusive possession of a small class; destructive criticism might be levelled at the theory, but that is not necessary or desirable if we only want to show how far morality may be improved by adequate housing. It is unfortunately too true that general brutality, traceable as a rule to drinking habits, plays a great part in the relations of the working classes; it is also true that bad housing

COTTAGES.

[*To face p.* 148.

lies at the root of these troubles. If we compare the police records of the Bebington district with those of Liverpool or London we are amazed, for of late years there has not been within the Port Sunlight district a single case of drunkenness nor a single case of wife beating. This alone should tend to show how enormous the improvement has been, for we have to deal in the Village with exactly the same class as in our city slums, viz. the unskilled labourer. It is a mistake to imagine that the houses are held mainly by superior artisans; they are mostly in the hands of men earning about 25*s.* a week—thus the above comparison may fairly be made. Wife beating is, however, so intimately connected with drunkenness that we can dismiss the two evils at the same time. Other forms of immorality, so prevalent in our industrial cities, are almost unknown in Port Sunlight. Amazing as it may seem in a community numbering about two thousand one hundred persons over fourteen, illegitimate births are of very rare occurrence in the Village. Of course it is impossible to keep count of such happenings, owing to the fact that women, when thus situated, often leave the district in which they are known, but given that the average rate of illegitimacy for Great Britain is about forty per thousand, and that there are between one hundred and one hundred and ten births every year in the Village, a proportion of the cases would necessarily come to light. No drunkenness, no wife beating, no immorality, no assaults, no deserted wives and children; is all this not an enviable record and a plea for an attempt to improve everywhere the living conditions of the people?

The normal result of sobriety and of cheap and

rational amusements is, of course, an increased tendency to provide for old age. Conscious of the fact that the pension fund will not help him if he ceases to be an employee of the Company, the Sunlighter is likely to set aside out of his small income as great a proportion as he can. Evidence of this tendency is forthcoming, for the Company, in order to encourage thrift, receives deposits from its employees at the rate of 4 per cent. per annum for every completed pound; these deposits amount on an average to £3500, or £30 per depositor. In other directions also economical habits are fostered or flourish without encouragement. I need only recall the fact that practically every adult employee subscribes to the Benefit Society; that the membership of the store amounts to some 80 per cent. of the number of householders; that almost all the employees have joined the Holiday Club. The contributions of the Company to the funds of the sick benefit society and the interest allowance to the Holiday Club are instances of intelligent and well-deserved support.

The foregoing characteristics, though material in their effects, are moral in their causes; there are, however, important results which are purely material in their origin. The chief of these are health and social conditions, for by these two alone we could almost judge the Village and approve or disapprove without going any further in our examination. It stands to reason that cleanliness, temperance, and open spaces must make for an improvement both in physique and general well-being, and it is important to show by means of comparison how great these improvements have been. The visitor is struck at once by the generally healthy appearance of the people and especially by the fine physique of the young men; the football team, for instance, is composed of young men in the twenties, and almost all the members of the team are notably taller and heavier than their local antagonists. The appearance of the children is remarkable, for they are usually fat, rosy, and irrepressibly cheerful; statistics referring particularly to them are quoted further on. Before dealing with the children, a few general statistics relating to the total population will go a long way towards demonstrating the excellent sanitary conditions prevailing in the Village.

VITAL STATISTICS.—It has been mentioned in the course of these chapters that the site on which Port Sunlight is built is low lying, and that much draining and damming had to be done to make it suitable for inhabitation. It might therefore be thought that the Village would not be healthy. The sanitary work has, however, been so thorough and the effects of good housing have been so marked that the average death rate of Port Sunlight compares very favourably with the figures for most other parts of the country.

Year.	Population.	Death rate per 100.
1900	2007	12·45
1901	2331	12·87
1902	2484	7·24
1903	2580	8.14
1904	2610	12·96
1905	2700	5·55
1906	2900	10·00
1907	3600	8·00
Average		9·00

It will be seen from the foregoing table that the death rate has fluctuated somewhat, as is inevitable in a small community where an epidemic may make all the difference; thus it is dangerous to instance any particular year, but fair to take the average of the last eight years, as a basis. The yearly report of the Registrar of Births, Marriages, and Deaths for England and Wales provides interesting comparisons with the Port Sunlight rate.

AVERAGE DEATH RATE PER 1000.

Denbighshire (highest county rate)	19
Carnarvonshire	18
Middlesex (lowest county rate)	11
76 great towns (over 50,000 inhabitants) ..	16·2
142 small towns (20,000 to 50,000 inhabitants)	14·7
Rest of England and Wales (country)	15
All England and Wales	16
Liverpool	20
Port Sunlight	9

This is a striking table, and it is apparent at once that the death rate of Port Sunlight is extraordinarily low; indeed hardly any individual towns have so low an average as Port Sunlight, except Hornsey (7 to 8), East Ham (8 to 9), and Willesden (8 to 9). Port Sunlight is apparently healthier than the healthiest county (11), than the English country districts (15); considerably healthier than the great towns (16·2) in which it would probably be the fate of the inhabitants to live and die, but for the model village. Here, therefore, we have already striking testimony to the advantages offered by life at Port Sunlight. Statistics of mortality must not, however, be taken as final; they must be analyzed with regard to infantile mortality.* It is indeed questionable whether it is worth while to prolong life indefinitely. I will not enter into a discussion of this thorny subject, but it is enough to say that a low general death rate is less important than a low rate of infantile mortality; thus it behoves us to compare Port Sunlight averages with those supplied in the registrar's report.

INFANTILE MORTALITY PER 1000. DEATHS IN FIRST YEAR OF LIFE.

Carnarvonshire (highest county)	160
Denbighshire	158
Oxfordshire	65
76 great towns (over 50,000 inhabitants) ..	125
Rest of England and Wales (excluding small towns)	97
All England and Wales	119
Liverpool	140
Dewsbury	179
Port Sunlight	70

Again Port Sunlight compares in a striking manner with all other parts of England. It is worth noting that its infant mortality is exactly half that of its immediate neighbour, Liverpool; given that the general death rate in Liverpool is more than double that of Port Sunlight, the four figures can be made the basis of a striking comparison. Can any one contend that a case has not been made for Port Sunlight in this

* Persons aged less than one year, according to the registrar's report.

respect also when its mortality rate for infants (70) is set beside the rate for all England (119)? The rate is beaten only by a few districts, such as Hornsey, Hastings, Bournemouth, etc.

SCHOOL CHILDREN OF LIVERPOOL AND PORT SUNLIGHT COMPARED.—The birth rate of Port Sunlight is equally satisfactory. It is not suggested that a high birth rate is a blessing, nor that it necessarily effects a condition of prosperity and culture, but, other conditions being good, a high birth rate may be taken to mean that the physical and mental health of the people is satisfactory. Before giving in this connection statistics which bear more especially on social relations, something should be said of the extremely interesting comparisons which have been made between Port Sunlight and Liverpool children. These figures were prepared on the one hand by Dr. Arkle for the Liverpool Education Committee,* and on the other by the Port Sunlight medical officer. It will be realized that these records are an important piece of evidence, and they are well worth detailed study. They concern five grades of Liverpool schools and the single grade of Port Sunlight elementary schools. According to Mr. Lever's paper read at the International Housing Congress at Port Sunlight on August 9 of 1907, these grades should be understood as follows:—

HIGHER GRADE SCHOOLS, where the sons of leading wealthy citizens are educated;

COUNCIL SCHOOLS "A."—Type of the best council school, where the parents of the children are

* In 1907, at the time of the sittings of the Royal Commissions on National Degeneration and the under-feeding of school children.

well-to-do, and the children have mostly comfortable homes;

COUNCIL SCHOOLS "B."—Type of school where the children are mostly of the labouring classes. Selected as a type for the children of the labouring classes whose parents have constant employment;

COUNCIL SCHOOLS "C."—A type of the poorest class, where the parents of the children belong almost entirely to the unemployed or casual labour sections;

PORT SUNLIGHT SCHOOLS may be taken as equivalent to type "B"; the parents belong mainly to the labouring classes but are in constant employment.

This being said, the following schedule of figures will be understandable:—

School.	6 Years.	6½ Years.	7 Years.	7½ Years.	8 Years.	8½ Years.	9 Years.	9½ Years.	10 Years.	10½ Years.	11 Years.	11½ Years.	12 Years.	12½ Years.	13 Years.	13½ Years.	14 Years.	
HEIGHT.	Ft. Ins.	Ft. Ins.	Ft. Ins.	Ft. Ins.	Ft. Ins.	Ft. Ins.	Ft. Ins.	Ft. Ins.	Ft. Ins.	Ft. Ins.	Ft. Ins.	Ft. Ins.	Ft. Ins.	Ft. Ins.	Ft. Ins.	Ft. Ins.	Ft. Ins.	Ft. I
Elementary Port Sunlight	3 6·91	3 8·04	3 9·74	3 10·70	3 11·51	4 0·5	4 1·19	4 2·67	4 2·41	4 4·75	4 4·36	4 5·00	4 6·24	4 6·84	4 8·46	4 7·47	5 0·75	5 2
Secondary Liverpool	..	3 11	3 11·4	4 1·83	4 2·61	4 2·5	4 4·03	4 4·37	4 6·41	4 6·83	4 7·50	4 8·87	4 10·00	4 9·40	5 0·55	4 11·77	5 1·75	5 3
Council School "A" Liverpool	..	..	3 9·33	3 10·70	3 11·67	3 11·62	4 1·76	4 1·75	4 3·30	4 3·70	4 5·11	4 6·25	4 6·90	4 7·50	4 9·05	4 8·62	4 10·2	4 8
Council School "B" Liverpool	3 7·25	3 6·75	3 8·80	3 8·17	3 10·0	3 11·33	4 0·80	4 1·61	4 1·70	4 3·04	4 3·80	4 4·53	4 5·60	4 6·34	4 5·90	4 7·23	4 8·25	·
Council School "C" Liverpool	..	..	3 8·00	3 10·00	3 8·37	3 9·20	3 11·00	4 0·0	4 0·50	4 0·75	4 1·75	4 2·30	4 3·60	4 4·16	4 5·6	4 6·55	4 7·25	·
Industrial School Liverpool	3 3·0	..	3 9·25	..	3 10·3	..	3 10·80	..	4 1·12	..	4 4·04	..	4 5·0	..	4 6·51	..	..	·
WEIGHT.	Lbs.	Lbs.	Lbs.	Lbs.	Lbs.	Lbs.	Lbs.	Lbs.	Lbs.	Lbs.	Lbs.	Lbs.	Lbs.	Lbs.	Lbs.	Lbs.	Lbs.	Lb
Elementary Port Sunlight	44·16	46·54	50·28	51·24	53·36	54·86	58·66	56·61	62·26	63·01	65·86	66·79	72·71	74·22	79·60	73·72	105·00	108·
Secondary Liverpool	..	48·0	49·30	56·70	56·70	52·50	59·52	640	66·03	68·76	70·27	74·75	77·05	74·00	88·25	85·72	94·5	108·
Council School "A" Liverpool	..	..	44·10	48·77	46·44	47·00	53·33	57·35	55·10	56·43	61·45	62·80	66·60	69·00	73·42	74·26	75·82	72·
Council School "B" Liverpool	37·00	36·50	43·00	42·11	45·64	47·20	50·85	53·16	53·00	56·60	59·05	60·79	63·92	67·50	68·75	68·50	75·87	·
Council School "C" Liverpool	..	..	43·00	46·00	43·87	45·30	48·38	51·50	..	54·37	55·50	58·30	62·05	63·73	69·33	70·63	71·14	·
Industrial School Liverpool	41·00	..	46·75	..	49·50	..	53·50	..	..	..	65·81	..	68·00	..	73·00	..	..	·

School.	6 Years.	6½ Years.	7 Years.	7½ Years.	8 Years.	8½ Years.	9 Years.	9½ Years.	10 Years.	10½ Years.	11 Years.	11½ Years.	12 Years.	12½ Years.	13 Years.	13½ Years.	14 Years.	
HEIGHT.	Ft. Ins.	Ft. Ins.	Ft. Ins.	Ft. Ins.	Ft. Ins.	Ft. Ins.	Ft. Ins.	Ft. Ins.	Ft. Ins.	Ft. Ins.	Ft. Ins.	Ft. Ins.	Ft. Ins.	Ft. Ins.	Ft. Ins.	Ft. Ins.	Ft. Ins.	Ft. I
Elementary Port Sunlight	3 6·13	3 8·02	3 8·81	3 9·61	3 9·31	4 0·09	3 11·41	4 0·37	4 2·36	4 4·31	4 3·97	4 5·32	4 6·90	4 8·37	4 9·63	4 11·32	5 0·25	5 0
Council School "A" Liverpool	..	..	3 10·75	3 10·13	3 11·50	4 0·25	4 2·62	4 2·25	4 3·25	4 2·75	4 5·00	4 4·75	4 7·25	4 9·00	4 8·30	4 10·75	5 0·50	5 1
Council School "B" Liverpool	..	3 8·00	3 8·25	3 9·77	3 10·73	3 10·57	4 0·25	4 1·20	4 1·76	4 3·35	4 4·12	4 4·25	4 5·70	4 6·14	4 7·30	4 8·87	4 5·70	4 10
Council School "C" Liverpool	..	..	3 9·12	3 8·73	3 8·87	3 9·50	3 11·16	4 0·00	4 0·17	4 0·30	4 1·06	4 2·70	4 4·16	4 5·16	4 7·50	4 7·00	4 8·50	.
Industrial School Liverpool	..	..	3 7·70	..	3 6·25	..	3 8·25	..	4 0·30	..	4 1·05	..	..	..	..	..	..	.

School.	6 Years.	6½ Years.	7 Years.	7½ Years.	8 Years.	8½ Years.	9 Years.	9½ Years.	10 Years.	10½ Years.	11 Years.	11½ Years.	12 Years.	12½ Years.	13 Years.	13½ Years.	14 Years.	
WEIGHT.	Lbs.	Lbs.	Lbs.	Lbs.	Lbs.	Lbs.	Lbs.	Lbs.	Lbs.	Lbs.	Lbs.	Lbs.	Lbs.	Lbs.	Lbs.	Lbs.	Lbs.	Lb
Elementary Port Sunlight	44·88	44·45	47·36	48·78	49·98	54·29	56·01	53·69	59·85	64·24	62·34	67·69	73·19	76·77	80·23	83·12	78·00	97·
Council School "A" Liverpool	..	..	43·00	44·6	48·85	50·00	52·00	52·85	57·50	55·46	61·28	60·70	71·31	77·30	70·30	80·50	93·30	97·
Council School "B" Liverpool	..	45·30	41·10	45·00	45·90	47·50	49·90	52·50	54·30	59·57	62·50	61·20	67·07	67·70	73·16	75·80	74·57	84·
Council School "C" Liverpool	..	..	47·00	50·00	44·16	46·70	48·50	50·05	52·75	53·20	56·25	60·57	67·70	69·12	73·30	74·00	82·00	..
Industrial School Liverpool	..	..	40·00	..	38·30	..	42·40	..	51·30	..	60·60	..	..	..	67·00	..	..	..

NOTE.—See section 1, page 158.

It is not unnecessary to comment upon the foregoing figures so as to crystallize conclusions, in view especially of the reservations embodied in the note appended to the schedule. Owing to a misunderstanding, or to prudishness on the part of parents, the Port Sunlight boys were weighed with more clothes than the Liverpool boys, so that results can be compared only by deducting two pounds from Port Sunlight weights. This deduction is, however, rather arbitrary, and it therefore appears preferable to confine the comparisons of weights to the girls, who were in both towns weighed in their everyday clothing. Heights are, of course, comparable in both cases and for both sexes, as they were taken in stockinged feet.

HEIGHT.—This is not a very important factor, for it has not much bearing upon the health of the people; it is good that a race should be tall and well-knit, but height is not a paramount consideration. Nevertheless it may be assumed that a tall child is fairly well developed; a few comparisons may therefore be useful; the figures allow for their being made to bear upon both sexes.

1. The Port Sunlight children are taller than those at present in industrial schools.

2. The Port Sunlight boys are taller than those in the highest class Liverpool Council schools; the girls are usually shorter than in Liverpool.

3. If we compare Port Sunlight boys and girls with type "B" (to which Sunlight schools closely approximate) we find that Port Sunlight boys are far in advance and that the girls almost equal their advantage.

4. The standards of Port Sunlight children are exceeded only by first-rate middle-class schools.

WEIGHTS.—These are, as has been said, interesting results, but the most valuable comparisons must be drawn from weights ; they are based exclusively on the girls, owing to the difficulties as regards the clothing of the boys, but they must apply equally well to both sexes.

1. Port Sunlight girls are between one and ten pounds heavier than those in the best Liverpool Council schools ; they are inferior at a few ages only.

2. They are anything up to thirteen pounds heavier than girls in Council School " B."

3. Comparisons with School " C " are irregular, but on the whole Port Sunlight girls are heavier.

4. Port Sunlight girls are as much as thirteen and fourteen pounds heavier than their fellows in industrial schools.

These are remarkable figures, all the more so when we remember that these large differences amount in some cases to 15 and even 20 per cent. of the children's total weight, and that 10 per cent. differences in favour of Port Sunlight are quite common. If we examine the records for the boys (keeping in mind the deduction for clothing) the results are equally remarkable.

1. Port Sunlight boys are beaten only by the middle-class schools.

2. They beat the best Council schools, in one case by thirty pounds.

3. Types " B " and " C " and the industrial school are also completely beaten.

I will only add a few striking facts, taking type " B " of the Council schools as a basis—

1. A Port Sunlight girl of seven and a half years is as heavy as a Liverpool girl of eight and a half.

2. A Port Sunlight girl of twelve and a half is much heavier than a Liverpool girl of thirteen and a half to fourteen.

These will suffice to show what a physical revolution has been worked in the children of the people by good food, good housing, open spaces, exercise, and regular employment of the parents. It is not too much to call it a revolution, for we must look to the children to perpetuate in their descendants the improvement of the race. In these days when our attention has at last been drawn to physical degeneration such figures are cheering, and they show us also our plain duty, whether we have it in our power to influence social conditions directly or only by means of a vote.

The results of the Port Sunlight *régime* have, however, made themselves felt in other directions. Regular employment, good housing, and all the advantages that follow in their train, influence something more than the health of the people: they have an important bearing upon their outlook. The Sunlighter, healthy and comparatively prosperous, has every inducement to marry early and to bring up a large family; his life is centred round his home and its simple pleasures, so that a large and well-reared family becomes a normal part of his economy. This question has been so fully and so ably dealt with by Mr. W. H. Lever himself in his paper at the International Housing Congress that I reproduce *in extenso* the portion that relates to this all-important marriage question—

"The following statistics relating to Port Sunlight have been drawn up by Mr. Duncan C. Fraser, the well-known actuary in Liverpool. Mr. Fraser took for his calculation those employees of Lever Brothers who, at the end of 1905, had seen ten years' service or over with the firm, their age and salary, married, widower, or single, and the number of children under the age of seventeen years. Every employee of ten years' service and over of the age of twenty-five or over was included, from the highest official to the lowest labouring man. On this clear basis Mr. Fraser divided the employees into six grades—

Lower Grade Workmen earning on the average £67 a year.

Higher Grade Workmen earning on the average £99 a year.

Lower Grade Clerks with an average income of £128 a year.

Higher Grade Clerks, being the higher section of the clerical staff, heads of departments, and men in positions of responsibility, the average earnings being £191 a year.

Lower Grade Business Men who were actually engaged in selling the products of the firm, the average income being £346 a year.

Higher Grade Business Men who were Directors, Managers, and Controllers, with salaries of over £1000 a year.

The above six grades, therefore, fall into three well-marked social divisions—Working-men, Clerks, and Business-men—and each division is sub-divided into lower and higher grades.

The following table gives the percentages of married men amongst these various grades:—

	Per cent.
Lower Grade Workman	78
Higher Grade Workman	96
Lower Grade Clerks	71
Higher Grade Clerks	66
Lower Grade Business Men	96
Higher Grade Business Men	92

The higher proportion of married men among the higher grade of working men is very striking, every man over the age of forty being married and having a wife living.

Mr. Fraser next compares the different grades with reference to the number of children. The children who were living and under the age of seventeen at the end of 1905 were classified according to the ages and grades of their fathers; and the *average* number of children *per married* man in each grade was found to be as follows:—

CHILDREN UNDER 17 PER MARRIED MAN.

Ages of Fathers.	Workman Lower Grade.	Workman Higher Grade.	Clerk Lower Grade.	Clerk Higher Grade.	Business Man Lower G.	Business Man Higher G.
25–29	1·0	1·7	0·4	1·0	—	—
30–34	2·0	2·7	1·0	2·0	1·0	1·7
35–39	2·9	3·5	1·7	1·5	1·7	2·5
40–44	2·6	4·1	—	—	1·2	2·5
45–49	3·1	2·9	2·0	2·0	2·2	1·6
50–54	2·9	2·9	—	6·0	1·0	2·2
55–59	0·4	1·0	—	1·0	—	—
60–69	—	—	—	—	—	—

From this table it will be seen that the higher grade of working man takes the lead in a most remarkable manner.

Mr. Fraser next calculated, taking the number of children per higher grade workman as the standard, the percentage there actually was in the other grades, and the result was shown to be as follows :—

PERCENTAGE OF CHILDREN UNDER 17 PER MARRIED MAN COMPARED WITH THE STANDARD OF CHILDREN OF HIGHER GRADE WORKING MEN.

	Per cent.
Working Men (Higher Grade)	100
„ (Lower Grade)	77·9
Clerks (Higher Grade)	61·1
„ (Lower Grade)	42·6
Business Men (Higher Grade)	62·4
„ (Lower Grade)	47·5

Mr. Fraser next considers the question of children from another point of view. The above table deals with the number of children per married man. Next, Mr. Fraser calculates the number of children per male employee in each of the above grades, whether the employee be married or single. This table, it will be noted, introduces as a further factor in the calculation the percentage of men unmarried at each grade. The result obtained in calculating the number of children under seventeen per man to each grade, taking the higher grade working man as the standard, was as follows :—

	Per cent.
Working Men (Higher Grade)	100
„ (Lower Grade)	65·2
Business Men (Higher Grade)	58·3
Business Men (Lower Grade)	46·8
Clerks (Higher Grade)	45·5
„ (Lower Grade)	33·0

Practically it will be seen that the male employees of all the other grades taken together rise only half-way to the standard set by the higher grade working men.

Mr. Fraser next prepared statistics in which the children are grouped in families, and the average number of children under seventeen per family arrived at was as follows:—

Working Men (Higher Grade)	3·1
„ (Lower Grade)	2·1
Business Men (Higher Grade)	1·8
„ (Lower Grade)	1·4
Clerks (Higher Grade)	2·0
„ (Lower Grade)	1·2

The preponderance of large families amongst the higher grade working men is very striking, and it was also found that more than half the children of the higher grade of working men were in families of more than four children. So far as Port Sunlight is concerned, it is clear that this is the grade which provides the increase of population. If Port Sunlight is representative of the general population of the United Kingdom, then we can assume that the increase of population—and, in fact, the great majority of the future population—will be provided by the higher grade of working men, the most intelligent and the fittest of their class, and we may take the most optimistic view of the future."

It only remains now to make a few comparisons between the general birth rate at Port Sunlight and the average in various parts of England. It will be gathered from the preceding figures that this rate must necessarily be high, and the fact is certainly not surprising in view of the high standard of comfort that prevails in the Village, and the human tendency to correlate the size of the family with that of the income. Let us, in the first place, give a table of the birth rates in the Village year by year.

Year.	Population.	Birth Rate per 1000.
1900	2007	48·33
1901	2331	51·48
1902	2484	39·45
1903	2580	52·71
1904	2610	47·90
1905	2700	42·70
1906	2900	35·86
1907	3600	30·0
Average ..	..	.. 42·0

In every case these averages exceed those of England and Wales. The birth rate has fluctuated a good deal, as it must in a small community; it is noticeable that it has been going down steadily of late years, but this phenomenon is not confined to the Village. At any rate, taking not the worst year, but what is fairer, the average of the last eight years, we find that the birth rate considerably exceeds English averages. This appears at once from an examination of the following comparative table :—

AVERAGE BIRTH RATE PER 1000.

Monmouthshire (highest county rate)	35·5
Durham	34·8
Sussex (lowest county rate)	21·3

76 great towns (over 50,000 inhabitants) ..	28·3
142 small towns (20,000 to 50,000 inhabitants)	26·9
Rest of England and Wales (country)	26·9
All England and Wales	27·5
Liverpool	33·7
Port Sunlight	42·0

This is eloquent testimony to the conclusions stated above and, in comparison with the numerous pieces of evidence that have already been quoted, it demonstrates what a powerful influence Port Sunlight has been as regards the prosperity and the development of the family, and how great a triumph is in store for the reformer who can level up living conditions on the lines followed by the founders of the Port Sunlight scheme.

CHAPTER IX

PART I

EDUCATION

EDUCATION, good or bad, is at one and the same time both a cause and a result of good or evil conditions. On the one hand, it is obvious that bad or insufficient education makes for a low standard of living, dirt, drunkenness, and immorality; on the other, that good education fosters most of the civic and private virtues. These are truisms, but it is important to realize that, where social conditions are bad, there can be no good, *i.e.* fruitful, education. It is therefore not surprising to find it on a high level at Port Sunlight. It should be clear that an ill-fed, ill-housed and overworked child cannot profit even if all the forces of pedagogy are brought into play; it must be equally clear that the Port Sunlight child, well-housed and nourished, sufficiently clad and rigidly debarred from half-time employment at the Works, must profit by its training to an extraordinary degree.

Everything that could make learning pleasant has apparently been done. The elementary schools, of which there are four—two for the infants, one for the juniors, and one for the seniors—are models of what schools should be. They were originally built and controlled by Messrs. Lever Brothers, but were taken over by the Cheshire County Council in pursuance of the Education Act (1902). They differ from the ordinary type of school in the peculiar features of their construction and in the spirit that informs the teaching. The buildings themselves are beautiful, built of bright red brick and covered with creepers; everywhere again we find large windows, abundant ventilation, perfect heating arrangements. The schools tell the same tale as all the other public buildings: hygiene, cheerfulness, and beauty. Each of the two schools * has a large hall, very high and Gothic in design. The walls of this hall are panelled in oak, distempered in white, and decorated with large reproductions of statuary, among which can be seen Apollo, Diana, Venus, etc. This is a welcome change from the over-common set of crude maps which completes the scene of desolation conjured up by rows of forms disfigured by ink stains and the knives of the small boys. At Port Sunlight we receive a very different impression, particularly if we have the good fortune to attend a class or the children's service in the large hall; these classes usually number fifty pupils, which is too much, but probably inevitable, unless the local expenditure on education is a good deal increased.

The staff consists of twenty-seven, of whom ten are uncertificated; they are fairly hard-worked, not so much because of the magnitude of the work itself, which means an average of forty pupils for every teacher, as because of the vitality of the children, which makes them distinctly unruly. The infants

* There are four schools, but they occupy only two buildings.

PARK ROAD SCHOOLS.

[*To face p.* 168.

especially are so healthy and strong as to be unmanageable at times; it's an ill wind, . . . and I suppose the teachers are not sorry at heart to find their charges so obstreperous. The school work follows the ordinary curriculum, so that it is unnecessary to say anything about the teaching itself, except that it is carried on under the best conditions.

The schools must, of course, admit as many children as the local authority may fix; thus the Port Sunlight schools, which were originally intended for Village children only, must now admit a number of outsiders. This is an excellent thing for the latter, and competition for entrance is keen, but a comparison between the physique and condition of Village and outside children reflects badly on the latter. The register bears the names of 1239 children, out of whom the average attendance for 1907 was 1046. This comprises 173 infants under five and 228 between five and seven, or together 40 per cent. of the total.

Control of the school is vested in the six managers, out of whom the local authority appoints as usual two, but it is interesting to note that Messrs. Lever Brothers have foregone their privilege of selecting four managers: they appoint only two, whilst the other two are elected by the villagers. Thus, though the schools were originally "voluntary," the people have the majority on the committee; it may be for this reason that there has never been any religious trouble at Port Sunlight. The teaching is undenominational, and is accepted by all the sects; indeed, up to the foundation of the Roman Catholic school at New Ferry, the children of the large Irish colony attended without a single protest. I do not want to fight the threadbare case of the so-called "Education" Bills over again, but it is permissible to wonder whether the quarrel is not one between "politicals," not between chapel- and church-goers.

It would be interesting to describe the Kindergarten held every Sunday, which is attended by some 400 serious infants, but it is impossible to convey an impression of the cordiality which pervades the proceedings. Ranged on tiny green-backed chairs sit the babes in solemn rows, singing simple hymns, cold-shouldering simple questions, or totally absent from the lesson, contemplating a visitor who is anxious to see them at work. The Kindergarten methods are at Port Sunlight followed with great success and with the best appliances; every child has its board and its sand tray, and there are many collective building and picture games. They were introduced and developed thanks to the efforts of the well-known expert, Mr. Archibald. Something must be said of the Cradle Roll, for it means a great deal in baby life at Port Sunlight. Every child is at birth entered upon this roll, and, on its first birthday, it is "received" by its seniors, the eldest of whom are not seven years old; the newcomer is admitted after one of his future companions has made him a friendly speech. This little institution is connected with the Sunday school, for which it hopes to make recruits, but its principal claim to notice is that it interests young children in their baby brothers and sisters, and links them together by investing with a ceremonial character the three successive celebrations of one another's birthdays, in which all take part; after the third birthday the "new boy" joins the Sunday school itself.

PARK ROAD SCHOOL CHILDREN.

[*To face p.* 170.

Attached to the elementary schools are the cookery and carpentry classes. When we consider the notorious want of management that prevails among so many working-class households, it is unnecessary to sing the praises of the first of these institutions. Every girl between the ages of eleven and fourteen is taught plain cooking, and also invalid and vegetable cookery, given a thorough knowledge of the dietary that is suitable for infants, of the use of the mangle, and fine laundry work. The classes are small, consisting as a rule of only eighteen girls, and are keenly interested. The wood-working class is compulsory for the boys between the ages of twelve and fourteen; they are taught the use of tools, the properties of various kinds of wood (mainly so as to develop their powers of observation), and are put to practical work, such as the making of boxes, knife-trays, simple articles of furniture, frames, etc. The class is excellently equipped, and much of the work is highly creditable, especially as all the articles manufactured by the boys are useful. The pupils are taken in small classes of not more than twenty, and are very keen.

As an encouragement to the children, Mr. Lever has for the last seven years given scholarships to the most promising boys and girls. Six are allocated every year, three to the boys and three to the girls; they allow the children to continue their studies at Secondary Schools. So far forty-four of these scholarships have been given, and there is keen competition for them.

Co-education prevails in all Port Sunlight schools. This system, which has so often been virulently attacked in this country, does not seem to have had at Port

Sunlight the dread moral and intellectual results foreshadowed by its opponents. Indeed, so far as can be judged from the appearance of the children and the statements of the teachers, co-education at Port Sunlight abundantly justifies the words of Mrs. Ennis Richmond—

"Under such a system girls learn to be women just as boys learn to be men, with a completeness and fulness utterly impossible under the ordinary system of separation."

Whether co-education or general excellence of buildings and system lies at the root of results, great compliments have been paid to the Port Sunlight schools, for the Chester Training College for Teachers and the Edgehill Training College, Liverpool, have approached the authorities with a view to taking visits of observation for their students.

Religious education is a feature at Port Sunlight. Various small organizations, such as the Bible Reading Association and the Bible Class connected with the Cricket Club, give up a good deal of time to the subjects, but the chief forces at work are, of course, the Boys' Brigade and the Sunday school. The brigade has over forty members, and would be much stronger if two rival bodies in the neighbourhood did not take toll of the Port Sunlight boys. Members pay 6*d.* a year and 6*d.* for a cap, the belt and haversack being supplied free. Over and above their weekly drill, the boys are trained in ambulance work, signalling, and shooting; all look clean and well set-up. They mostly attend a Sunday morning Bible Class under their captain and a helper, though they are not compelled to do so.

CHURCH DRIVE SCHOOLS.

[*To face p.* **172.**

The Sunday school itself is an important organization, for it has over 1000 members, or 65 to 70 per cent. of the Village children. So large is it that it has been divided into three departments, and runs classes totalling 500 children at a time. The school trains its own teachers, who are recruited from among young men and girls of fifteen to sixteen; in spite of the fact that the duties are somewhat onerous, and that no reward is attached to the position, the application list is always full. A number of Sunday evening lantern services are held throughout the winter. Before passing on to the Technical Institute, we should mention that some twenty Port Sunlight scholars (mainly boys) have passed on to training colleges, and are now fully certificated teachers in public elementary schools.

The Technical Institute, a gift of Mr. Lever's, has become the seat of the Bebington Centre. It is a fine building situated at the most northern point of the estate, contiguous to New Ferry, and easily accessible from Bebington. Technical centres often suffer from lack of space, but the institute has the great advantage of being large enough to accommodate all the classes at the same time. The fees for training are in all cases low, 2*s.* 6*d.* to 10*s.* per annum, and a large number of free studentships are granted to regular attendants. The course covers three years, and all classes are, of course, held in the evening. A notable point is that the committee has introduced "compulsory guidance" of the students; instead of allowing the latter, as is too often done, to study as much, or as little, as they choose, it now compels them to select a group of subjects, and to attend regularly under penalties, such as fines (if the student does not attend at fourteen lessons in each subject), or even suspension. At the end of the three years' course the most promising students receive scholarships which take them to higher centres in Liverpool, Birkenhead, or Chester; by this means technical education may be prolonged to five years in all. Examinations are held by the Lancashire and Cheshire Union of Technical Institutes, which delivers certificates; certain classes also prepare the student for the examination of the Board of Education (Science and Art Department).

The curriculum is wide. It comprises a full knowledge of commercial arithmetic, economic geography, business methods and correspondence, shorthand (one hundred and twenty) and typewriting, book-keeping and accountancy, French, German, mathematics and practical draughtsmanship, general physics, geometry (including solids), elementary trigonometry, mechanics (theoretical and applied), building and machine construction, wood-carving, freehand drawing, needlework, dressmaking, cookery, domestic economy, sick nursing, and ambulance work. This is an extensive programme, and it is therefore not surprising that the attendance should average five hundred.

In connection with higher education a most interesting departure has lately been made at Port Sunlight, which shows how much value is attached to the mental development of the workers. It was announced in June, 1908, that from July 1 onwards, no employee under eighteen would be engaged unless he or she should have attained a specified standard in the schools. Furthermore, all employees between the

SCHOOLS : MAIN HALL.

[*To face p.* 174.

ages of fourteen and eighteen are henceforth, as a condition of their employment, to attend evening continuation schools. These rules are now in force for existing employees between the ages of fourteen and sixteen and are optional for those at present between the ages of sixteen and eighteen; in both cases the total cost of education will be defrayed by the Company. This is an important innovation, for we know only too well how insufficient, and how unsatisfactory, is the education which a child can obtain before the age of fourteen; it is certain that this wise and generous scheme will be fraught with momentous results. If the conditions of labour were in all industrial centres as good as they are at Port Sunlight, it would be a good thing to establish these schools on a compulsory legal basis. Young persons are, however, not everywhere so well housed, and so well fed, as they are in the Village, and we must therefore be content with such partial improvement as that which will result from this enlightened piece of initiative.

This necessary survey of education is far too short to show how thoroughly, and in how many directions, the child is cared for in a city of ideas which is also a city of ideals, but that is unavoidable. A result and a cause in one—education is doing for Port Sunlight a great and good work. It is worth observing that one unconsciously returns at the end of this survey to the train of thought which ran through its first part, that the effects of education, and the determining factors of education, react so intimately upon one another as to leave one wondering whether it will bring about the millennium, or more humbly follow in its sumptuous train.

PART II

THE PORT SUNLIGHT SPIRIT

It appears clearly enough from the foregoing pages that the influence of Port Sunlight has been something more than healthful and educational. The little community lives however under such unusual conditions, so many of its citizens have lived there for ten years or more and so many, now growing up, have been born within its limits, that a something, intangible and peculiar, seems to have moulded the character of the Sunlighters into a novel shape. Many sidelights and digressions in the course of the preceding chapters must to a certain extent have given a clue to the attitude of the people, but this was necessarily done in haphazard and piecemeal fashion; it may be well, therefore, to return to the subject in detail.

It must be obvious, too obvious, that the people of our slums have been influenced by their terrible surroundings, that evil conditions have sometimes degraded them so far as to falsify their tradition of humanity. It is, therefore, permissible to say that good conditions must have modified to a commensurate degree those who have been so fortunate as to settle in the Village. Experience confirms, besides, that which theory dictates; it cannot be denied that local influence has been at work at Port Sunlight, and that the community is developing a type with clear-cut qualities and defects. Obviously this influence must grow, and with it will increase the characteristics of the Port Sunlight type.

This process, normal enough in the counties and in large cities such as London or Manchester, is rather unusual in small towns: there is no St. Albans type, no Westcliff type. In Port Sunlight, however, conditions are so different from those of the immediate neighbourhood that it is almost possible to identify the inhabitants, and even more possible to identify the children.

Some of the more outstanding characteristics, the purely external, have been reviewed in Chapter VIII. Thus it is enough to recall the ever-present feeling that Port Sunlight has erected a shrine for the worship of cleanliness; spotless streets, trim gardens, white curtains, such is the impression that the visitor inevitably carries away with him, whether he remain in the Village for two hours or two weeks. Among the cottages I visited, all thoroughly clean, there is one which will remain impressed upon my memory. Its rental is 5*s.* 3*d.* a week (including rates), and it is at present occupied by a labourer earning 23*s.* a week; his family consists of his wife and two daughters who are too young to work, and he has no room for a lodger. The benefit society absorbs 9*d.* a week, so that the family has to deal with a balance of only 17*s.* a week. This very narrow income has to provide for the food, fuel, clothing, recreation, and incidental expenses of two adults and two children: by what prodigies of economy this is achieved I do not pretend to say; the fact, however, remains that the house is a home in the best sense of the word, and that the family is undisguisedly happy. In the living-room is good and far from tasteless furniture; some fifty books occupy the shelves of a small bookcase; the boards are scrubbed, the tiles obviously well rinsed, the curtains white. The atmosphere is restful with that restfulness that tells of hard work done to obtain it, but everywhere content and happiness, its fair fruit, make their presence felt. These people are poor, but they have retained or regained their "humanhood": the parents are kindly and courteous; the children are well mannered and well spoken, and have developed a family taste for music. A singular sweetness breathes from the tiny home when the father returns and the day's work is done.

The atmosphere of peace is felt everywhere, for the Sunlighters are a sedate race. The wonderful organization of the Village, its readiness for all emergencies and all individualities, have reacted upon the people, have made them sober and deliberate beyond even the standards of the North. Regularity and method seem to make the leisure of the people as ordered as their labour; self-imposed though it be, their discipline is strict, and they seem ideally fitted by their residence in a model community to become one day dwellers in an ideal state.

There is no unrestrained youth in Port Sunlight; the offensive vulgarity that grates upon us in so many of our industrial cities seems altogether absent. The barbarian that lives equally in the London hooligan and in the undergraduate is either kept well in check or has never developed. Perhaps the Port Sunlighter knows of no bounds—perhaps he is ideally free: at any rate, he does not seem to chafe, to nurse the everlasting desire of some of our youth to shout, throw stones, or fall foul of the police. Indeed, one cannot help being impressed, especially on Sundays, by the

THE SUNDAY SCHOOL. [*To face p.* 178.

power that has made the villager into the quiet, orderly citizen that he is.

Sedate and well disciplined as he is, the Port Sunlighter must owe a great deal to the atmosphere of morality and piety that he drinks in at every breath. The North supplies most of our enthusiasts, our dreamers and leaders: here, the men of the North, with an admixture of neighbouring Welsh and Irish Celts have not belied but more than justified their reputation. The Sunlighter impresses one as more deeply but more reasonably religious than is the case with members of many other communities; a service at Christ Church is interesting if only because of the large number of men who attend. Wherever religion is dying, whether by its own narrowness or its sterility, we find that it is men who first desert its ranks; the women, last defenders of lost causes, remain to the end. Thus, wherever we find a church whose congregation consists almost entirely of women, we have a dying church; it is far from my intention to compare unfavourably the value to a church of a woman as opposed to that of a man, but a preponderance of either sex is always a sign. At Port Sunlight the male portion of the congregation is large and earnest. The people are always ready to come to services, to make their religion a truly living thing; in fact, they vindicate by the fact of their existence the value of "a church for the comfortable," for to them it is as much as to their poorer brethren, if not more.

Bound up with religion is morality, and it is significant that they go hand in hand. Religious feeling, or rather devoutness, singularly enough, does not always make for purity of life, as is shown by the standards which prevail in Southern Europe. In England, on the other hand, morality and religious feeling are usually found together, and nowhere are they more closely allied than at Port Sunlight. Standards are certainly wonderfully rigid in the little town; the "oldest inhabitant" could only recall one elopement and in 1907 there was only one illegitimate birth, or about four times less than the average for Great Britain; during the last dozen years only two persons have been involved in what may be called a village scandal. These are truly remarkable facts, and show, in regard to what we know of industrial conditions and of the holocaust of souls that is revealed every day in our police courts, what a revolution has been worked in the habits of the people. This revolution is, as has already been said, traceable in great part to sobriety. The connection that exists between temperance, good housing, and morality is powerful though elusive; so much, however, has already been said on this subject in the foregoing chapters that it is enough to place on record that the spirit of Port Sunlight is one of sobriety and self-restraint.

All this might lead us to think that these religious, moral, sober, and sedate men and women represent a rather hard and narrow type. We might expect to find the Sunlighter puritanical, and he does not entirely escape the imputation. It is possible that he is rather pronounced in his virtues, that something of the spirit of New England breathes in him, but if this be in truth a newer England then let us hope that the movement begun at Port Sunlight will not slacken. Puritanically inclined though he may be the

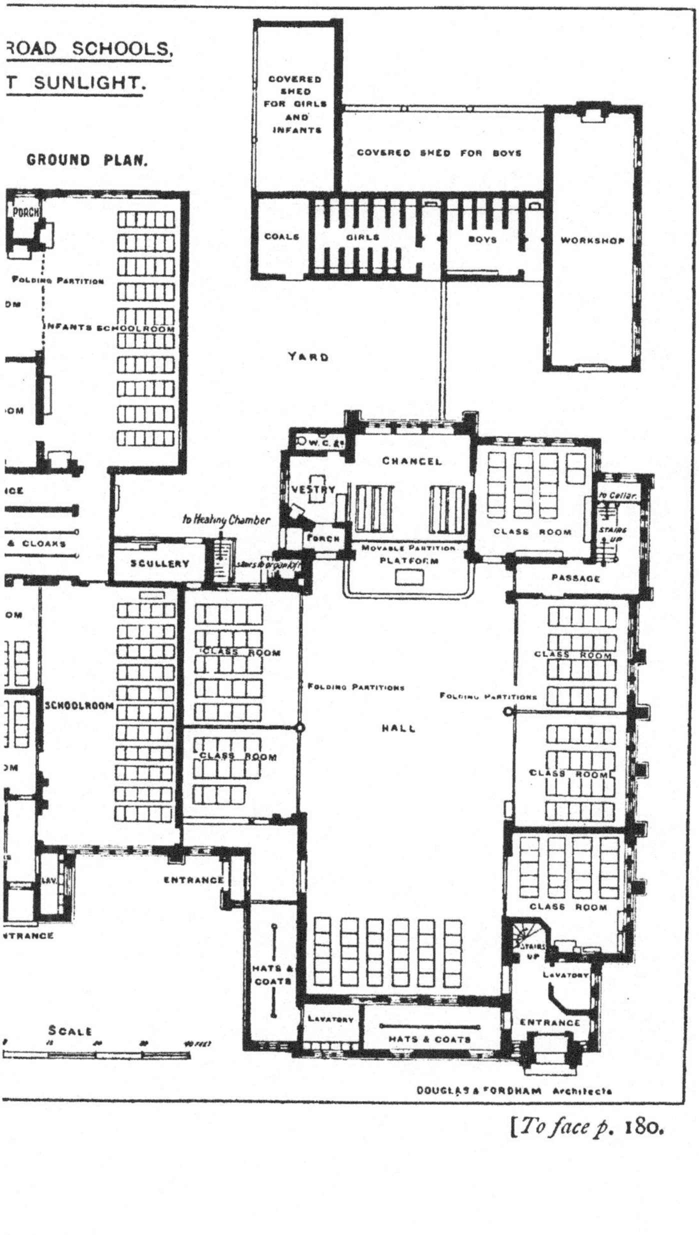
ROAD SCHOOLS,
T SUNLIGHT.
GROUND PLAN.
COVERED SHED FOR GIRLS AND INFANTS
COVERED SHED FOR BOYS
COALS
GIRLS
BOYS
WORKSHOP
YARD
PORCH
FOLDING PARTITION
INFANTS SCHOOLROOM
W.C. &c
CHANCEL
VESTRY
CLASS ROOM
to Cellar.
STAIRS UP
to Heating Chamber
PORCH
MOVABLE PARTITION
PLATFORM
& CLOAKS
SCULLERY
PASSAGE
SCHOOLROOM
CLASS ROOM
FOLDING PARTITIONS
HALL
CLASS ROOM
ENTRANCE
LAV.
HATS & COATS
LAVATORY
HATS & COATS
STAIRS UP
LAVATORY
ENTRANCE
SCALE
DOUGLAS & FORDHAM Architects

[*To face p.* 180.

Sunlighter has not given up innocent pleasures; he has not become hard or intolerant. As far as can be judged from undenominational services and teaching, freedom in library and reading-rooms, the character of lectures, etc., the effort of the community is towards breadth and light. For this breadth of spirit some credit is due also to the important excursions which are organized from time to time at Port Sunlight. A community which has been transported bodily to Paris, to Liège, to the Franco-British Exhibition, etc., has enjoyed some of the enlarging experiences of travel and knowledge of the world beyond its own local surroundings. This community cannot help being influenced by comfort, any more than it can help aiming at it, but while it escapes over-spiritualization it does not become materialistic. In fact, it is neither puritanical nor anti-puritanical: it is well regulated and, intellectually speaking, emphatically sane and well balanced. The virtue of cheerfulness, so alien to the severer forms of worship, is everywhere flourishing, for the Sunlighter who clearly makes a business of work also makes a business of pleasure. Dances, picnics, lectures, and entertainments of all sorts follow in rapid rotation, so that the community remains young in its appreciation of pleasure as a necessity.

In no direction is cheerfulness so apparent as in the case of the children. The little folk have not escaped the influence that works on their elders: the infants are too healthy not to be unruly, but their seniors between the ages of six and fourteen give the visitor a curious impression of discipline and self-control. They are not repressed: their ideas flow quickly, but their general tone is one both thoughtful and cautious. Their northern ancestry is of course partly responsible for their sober outlook, but education and favourable conditions have directed into the channels of thought tendencies that evil surroundings would have exaggerated into dourness. And no wonder, for the most outstanding trait of the Port Sunlight spirit is the love borne to the children. The child is the primary care of the Sunlighter, his hobby, his most sacred responsibility; indeed, this community probably echoes a sentiment expressed to me by one of the men in the Village: "We must do all we can for those under sixteen." This great task is safe in the hands that control it, for the young and the weak are not forgotten at Port Sunlight. The care, the quasi-pampering bestowed on the girls as opposed to the sterner treatment of men is an evidence of this concern for the weak; the community thinks well of cheap food, free transit, free baths, free meals, etc., for the girls, because they need these advantages, and who will deny it? The result of all this is obvious: the weak are passing strong and natural disabilities are redressed. Nowhere do we see ragged or bootless children—the under-fed child is almost unheard of—indeed, the younger section is so remarkably living, vital, devoid of shyness, that it makes nothing of stopping the stranger in the street and engaging him in interminable though elementary conversations.

Such tendencies as these go naturally with the appreciation of home life. The Sunlighters are a stay-at-home race: indeed, in the evening they seem to disappear. One may find half a dozen men at the inn, perhaps thirty at the club, probably a hundred or

CHILDREN AT A DRILL CLASS.

[*To face p.* 182.

so at various meetings, but the remaining 3400 odd souls remain at home. By ten, or before it, the streets are deserted, and the lights which as the sun went down appeared in the windows are one by one extinguished and the Village sleeps. Hard work, simple and thoughtful pleasures—is not such an ideal worth striving after and cherishing?

The Sunlighters work hard, but they are also inclined to play hard. The spirit of the Village is one of keenness and activity; things done and things in the doing are everywhere to be seen and every one is convinced that the earth revolves round the axis of his own personal interest. Nowhere is this more apparent than in the societies, whose secretaries are one and all dominated by the ambition of seeing their charges become not only prosperous but larger than any other society. It would be invidious to quote instances, but there is keen competition among the athletic societies and the intellectual societies to secure new members. The two groups stand aloof from one another, each one taking up an attitude of superiority, but inside each group competition is fierce; teachers, nurses, officials, are all equally keen. Anything healthier or more conducive to a good mental tone cannot be imagined: the societies keep one another up to the mark. Thus every secretary seems certain that his society is of all the most vigorous, or the most promising, or the most intelligent, etc. This spirit has fostered in the Sunlighters both sociability and democratic feeling. It would be a lengthy and not very useful piece of work to find out exactly how many of the inhabitants are members of one society or more, but the total membership of the institutions for adults (excluding the stores and the benefit society as purely business concerns) is about 2500.* Of these a certain number are outsiders, but the total is highly satisfactory as showing that of about 1700 persons over twenty-one living in the Village, every man or woman in Port Sunlight is on an average a member of more than one society. There is no doubt that this large membership means continual association between the villagers—meetings, dances, picnics, etc., where they can exchange ideas; thus the spirit of sociability, inimical to suspicion and prejudice, seems to breathe among the people and makes them fit for the boon of democratic government.

At Port Sunlight democracy is, at the same time, living and quiescent. On the one hand, owing to the fact that the estate is managed as is usual on private property, but still more so because the tenants are employees of the landlord, democracy is not very active; tenants have no voice in the making of rules, nor have they any voice in the management of the estate. There is no special reason to complain especially of this, for such is the position on most private estates, with this difference, that the management is almost disinterested, and that its only care is the comfort of the tenants. Besides, the latter have their urban district council vote and can powerfully influence local administration. On the other hand, democratic feeling seems strong because the people are being trained in self-government by means in great part of their societies. Thus it is not surprising to find them wide awake and ready to attend political

* This takes no account either of trade unions, friendly societies, or the holiday club.

meetings in a controversial spirit. Should their aptitude for further democratic government ultimately be put to the test by the institution of an advisory council there is very little reason to think that they will not rise to their task.

The last and prominent feature of the spirit of Port Sunlight lies in that most important factor of industrial institutions: good feeling between employer and employee. It is not too much to say that at Port Sunlight Mr. W. H. Lever's ideal "to socialize and Christianize business relations" has been attained. By its achievements in that respect the scheme stands or falls. It is unfortunately too true that the relations between Capital and Labour have assumed the shape of an armed truce, a truce which is every day broken by strikes and lock-outs. Such a state of things was inevitable as industry passed more out of the hands of the small employer and into those of powerful combinations owned by absentee shareholders. Contact between employer and employee having been interrupted or rather restricted to the sole medium of a manager who is as much part of the dividend-earning machinery as is the engine in the boiler-room, mutual interest naturally disappeared. Thus vanished those palliatives of mutual interest, work in common, and friendliness which alone justify the holding in trust of private enterprises. In the words of Mrs. Besant* "the denial of human sympathy by the employer in his business relations with his 'hands,' has taught the 'hands' to regard the employer as outside the pale of their sympathy." It is against this tendency, against this fatal result of modern industrial practice,

* Fabian Essays, "Industry under Socialism."

that the founders of Port Sunlight have sallied out, and the spirit of the Village fully justifies their efforts.

When I was at Port Sunlight I interviewed a number of men and women of all ranks, some of whom were drawing the *minimum* wage of 22*s.* or but little more. Close cross-questioning never elicited anything but expressions of cordial feeling towards Mr. Lever and his co-directors. The inhabitants mostly remember other and less favoured spots, and are keenly conscious of the benefits they derive from their residence in the Village. Moreover, they recognize how good are the conditions under which they labour and gratefully acknowledge their excellence. The spirit of the Village is, however, something more. To accept benefits and to be thankful for them is well, but if such a feeling were all, it is not certain that the inhabitants ought altogether to be congratulated, for they would only be accepting patronage. There is, however, evidence of the existence of a closer relation between employer and employees, of personal acquaintance and personal liking. This is shown in many ways, every one small, yet every one important.

Contact between masters and men is frequent at Port Sunlight; formerly it was still closer, for Mr. Lever was chairman of the various Village institutions' committees, but these have now grown so numerous that the alternative was either favouritism and consequent jealousy or an undue amount of work, so that he had to resign these positions. Nowadays, however, Mr. Lever, his co-directors, and the general manager frequently assist at lectures and meetings; they also go to all the important entertainments. A small incident at one of the weekly dances went far to convince me of the excellence of the relations between employers and employees. It was a very large dance given to the girls in the soap-packing department, and was attended by Mr. Lever, his family, and the general manager. One of the young girls came up to the latter and, reminding him that it was leap year, asked him to be her partner, which he, of course, did at once. Could such an incident take place if relations were not thoroughly cordial? I was informed also by a young foreman that Mr. Lever himself would certainly have been approached without hesitation if he had not left the hall at that moment. Similar signs of personal interest were noticeable also at the women's guild, the meetings of which are frequently attended by the families of the directors.

All this goes to show that Port Sunlight has done more than house its inhabitants well; the good conditions of labour and the contact between the different grades have gone far towards combating prejudice and class antagonism. It is therefore not too much to say that the Port Sunlight spirit, this new and more Christian feeling, is one of the fairest fruits of the system. The spectacle of loyal co-operation in labour, mutual trust and liking, and above all the understanding of the differences of outlook due to pecuniary circumstances, are most encouraging when we remember how great and threatening is the gulf that separates those who own the instruments of production from those who use them. Perhaps, if the lesson be read by other men, evolution may lead us on somewhat similar lines towards a culmination when that which is the best and the truest of life will be enjoyed by all men alike.

PART III

OPINIONS

Port Sunlight has been the subject of a number of chapters in various books, of many references in large works, and of so many magazine articles, that it is not uninteresting to inquire into the impression made by the Village and the Works upon some of the authors. Before doing this, I would refer the reader to Part II. of the present chapter for the opinion of the men, and to the next chapter for that of the employer. We must remember that by reason of the large number of trade unions, the members of which are employed at the Works, it has been found impossible to obtain anything like a general opinion. Facts, however, speak for themselves; the northern branches are not given to leaving their members in distress, and it is certain that they would have been up in arms if occasion had arisen. It is therefore enough to repeat that, thanks to good conditions, fair treatment, and a *minimum* wage which is never below, and often above, trade union rates, there has never been at Port Sunlight either a strike or the menace of a strike. This fact certainly speaks volumes, and goes far to establish firmly the reputation as employers of the founders of Port Sunlight.

Among the social students who have visited and written of Port Sunlight, let us note Mr. Vallenda, whose important German work contains many complimentary references to the Port Sunlight system, and M. Georges Benoit-Lévy, whose book on Garden Cities (in French) has attracted a great deal of attention. As it is more recent than Mr. Vallenda's (it was published in 1904), a few of his remarks are well worth quoting. M. Benoit-Lévy devotes about thirty pages to Port Sunlight; this, of course, gives only a general idea of the scheme, but it very successfully outlines its most important social and financial features. M. Lévy seems very favourably impressed with the Village, of which he says (according to a translation in pamphlet form):

"One must have travelled a little in England and visited the industrial English towns to understand the surprise which the sudden appearance of Port Sunlight produced. One feels as if leaving the towns of the Devil and suddenly entering the Garden of Eden."

This, perhaps, puts the case rather strongly, for Port Sunlight is hardly a fairy land, where the inhabitants live lives of leisure and "drink the subtle Azzigoom." Our author also fully realizes the value of communal life. Speaking of Hulme Hall he says:

"There is no doubt that the people, who are in constant contact with one another, develop a different kind of individuality to individuals who lead an isolated and secluded life. Now, thanks to the constant and daily contact, the sense of sociability has a magnified scope of development."

M. Lévy was particularly enthusiastic over the athletic societies, which is natural enough when we consider the small extent to which these have hitherto developed in France, but he seems more deeply interested rather in the Port Sunlight idea than in its embodiment. He criticizes the government of the community as being too autocratic, but he seems entirely in sympathy with "prosperity-sharing," as opposed to "profit-sharing." He sums up his general opinion of the Village in enthusiastic terms:

"It is certainly the best of the kind we have seen. We have visited numerous working men's colonies where the houses are supplied by the employers, but we never came across an organization which was so perfect from every point of view."

The reader of the subject-matter of the foregoing pages will surely agree that there are good grounds for M. Benoit-Lévy's approval.

Among British works on social subjects we may note "Housing Up-to-date," by Alderman W. Thompson, the premier authority on the matter. In this book Alderman Thompson does not devote very much space to Port Sunlight, for he aims above all at producing a convenient compendium of information, and his is an enormous subject. He appears much impressed by the statistics with regard to the health of the children; in his opinion:

"Nothing is more striking in the village than the care and interest manifested towards the children, and the happy results that have followed."

Mr. Thompson is also much interested in the licensing of Bridge Inn, and appears to accept this development with equanimity. Thus:

"Those responsible for the good government and

management of the Village have assured the writer that the change has been beneficial rather than otherwise to the social and moral well-being of the inhabitants."

Lastly, let us quote a few remarks from "Model Factories and Villages," by the late Mr. Budgett Meakin, who probably knew more about conditions of labour than any man of his period. Mr. Meakin comments on the industrial conditions of the Factory, on the free trains, shower-baths, etc. He is also much impressed by the size and efficiency of Hulme Hall, the extent of the club grounds, and the library. He is of opinion that "the suggestion boxes provide an admirable stimulus." Mr. Meakin's observations are scattered throughout his book, which makes it difficult of quotation, but it is interesting to put on record that he thinks the schools "splendidly fitted," the public hall "a model of convenience and simplicity for any village," and the inn "most attractive."

In fact, it is almost impossible to find in any authoritative work condemnation of the objects pursued at Port Sunlight, or of the methods applied to attain them; minor criticisms, such as those which occur in these chapters, are made by various authors, some justified, some rather prejudiced, but the consensus of opinion is so strongly in favour of Port Sunlight that one almost fears to quote too abundantly for fear of being carried away and indulging in dithyrambics. If, however, we consider the foregoing facts one by one, we are driven to agree with the common judgment of these social students, and to accept the Village as the nearest approach to ideal conditions.

CHAPTER X

PROFIT AND LOSS

THE foregoing chapters must have conjured up an idyllic picture, and I will not overload it with colour. It is permissible to say that the Village is, from the point of view of the employee, an ideal institution—that it gives him most of those things that make life worth living—that it sows in him the seeds of moral and physical health. There is, however, another and perhaps more important point of view, for nowadays we too often find that an appeal in the sacred name of humanity is ineffectual, whilst the prospect of gain is always attractive ; that is the employer's point of view. For him the value of a social scheme must be summed up in two questions: "What does it cost?" and "Does it pay?"

In a sense the value of a scheme and its future prospects must be gauged by the answers to those two questions. A social venture cannot be called social unless it is going to pay its way. In an imperfect civilization, where the distribution of land is bad and the regulation of industry non-existent, sheer philanthropy is a necessity. It is true that philanthropy creates the evil it relieves, but we cannot sweep it away until a constructive social policy has enabled us to minimize if not to destroy the evils against which it struggles. If, therefore, a social scheme is to avoid making half a dozen paupers for every man it rescues, if it is to rise from the level of a necessary evil to that of a working part of the world's machinery, its basis must be a practical understanding. A social scheme should show credits as well as debits ; we do not expect to earn profits from housing or land policies, but we do expect these ventures to show, by defraying the bulk of their own cost, that they are both necessary and vigorous. Thus a municipal tramway scheme is good if it pays, bad if it does not ; this must be understood broadly, for payment can be made in coin or in kind ; the Thames steamboats did not pay in cash, but it can be argued that they paid in convenience or pleasure, like a museum or a park.

If, however, we abandon the analogy of public social schemes and confine ourselves to private ventures the position somewhat alters. Whereas it is obviously in the interest of the community to promote the well-being of its component parts, it is apparently in the interest of the individual to promote nothing but his own. This is a grim and sordid view, but facts must be faced, if we are to think clearly ; the manufacturer does not run a factory merely for the purpose of employing workmen. It is for this reason that it becomes all important to determine whether such a scheme as Port Sunlight pays. If it pays it is a great scheme, for its profits are not gained at the expense of the workers ; if it does not pay, then it is bounty-fed and demoralizing.

Before attempting to ascertain whether Port Sunlight pays it is important to see what it costs. At first sight this appears easy, but funds flow out in so many ways that it is difficult to arrive at exact figures. Roughly, however, we find that at the present time the profits of the soapworks are, subject to deductions, worth about £35,000 a year.* This large amount is made up of the following items :—

	£	s.	d.
Old Age Pensions (1907)	8,000	0	0
Interest contribution (1907)	24,680	10	0
Interest and Amortization on Church and Technical Institute, Contributions to Benefit Society, Interest allowances, etc., say	3,000	0	0

Some of these items have already been dealt with. The cost of the old age pension scheme is not quite within the scope of this discussion; it is a compassionate allowance, and as it comes after the worker's career is ended it does not, in theory, affect his labour very much. The influence it may have is indirect; in a sense it places him in a position to abstain from saving, and encourages a higher standard of living, but this is far from absolute; the worker who would rely on the firm's old age pension, though in a position to save a little himself, would not be worth helping. He would be showing himself improvident, for the old age pension is a privilege, not a right—a privilege he would forego if he left the Works. Besides, the old age pension is not large, and the worker must supplement it himself. It appears, therefore, that this form of prosperity-sharing does not affect the question very

* Including the value of Mr. Lever's personal gifts to the community.

much. The same may be said of the item of £3000. The Church and the Technical Institute are gifts of Mr. Lever; in a sense they also are part of the prosperity-sharing, but many rich men who have not introduced any schemes of this nature have also showered gifts upon certain localities. If, therefore, we take £25,000 as being about the sum which is specifically subtracted from profits for the purpose of assisting the Village account, we shall have an approximately correct idea of the cost to the firm of the Village itself.

Given that this sum of £25,000 is handed over to the community of villagers, their balance sheet can be *roughly* summed up as follows:—

PORT SUNLIGHT VILLAGE.

Dr.	£	Cr.	£
Income from rents, etc.	8,000	Expenditure	33,000
Prosperity-sharing ..	25,000		
	£33,000		£33,000

These £25,000, being handed to the community, the question then arises: "How should it be handed over?" The value of the bonus being calculated at an average of £8 for every employee, the logical answer would be, "Pay every employee an average of £8." That would be profit-sharing in its crude form, and with such a course would be bound up all the evils discussed at length in Chapter I. I will not return to the subject, but must quote the opinion of Mr. Lever himself, as expressed in an interview he gave M. Benoit-Lévy* in 1903, in the following terms:—

"If I were to follow the usual mode of profit-sharing I would send my workmen and work girls to the cash office at the end of the year and say to them: 'You are going to receive £8 each; you have earned this money; it belongs to you. Take it and make whatever use you like of it. Spend it in the public-house; have a good spree at Christmas; do as you like with your money.' Instead of that I told them: '£8 is an amount which is soon spent, and it will not do you much good if you send it down your throats in the form of bottles of whisky, bags of sweets, or fat geese for Christmas. On the other hand, if you leave this money with me, I shall use it to provide for you everything which makes life pleasant, viz. nice houses, comfortable homes, and healthy recreation. Besides, I am disposed to allow profit-sharing under no other than that form.'"

This is a clear, if blunt, statement of the case, and little need be added to it. It does not yet, however, reveal to us the employer's point of view; it only shows us the man who wishes to do the best he can for his workers, not the man who wants to make them productive. These aims are, however, there, and Mr. Lever is at pains to assure and to show us that he is no philanthropist. The idea grows interesting when we are assured that "it pays." Briefly, the objects of Port Sunlight are as follows:—

1. To establish friendly relations between Capital and Labour.
2. To get the men to do their best work.

* See "The Garden City," by Georges Benoit-Lévy.

3. To make the men's comfort depend on the firm's prosperity.
4. To put Capital in the right by treating the men as well as possible, leaving it to their conscience to repay.

It will be seen from this that the idea of a return underlies the whole scheme. It is, of course, very difficult to prove that more soap and better soap is produced because the men are well housed; but it is clear that there is a strong *primâ facie* case to support the founder's expectations. It is easy to point to the enormous and growing profits of the soapworks, and to conclude that this state of things is due to the existence of the Village; but such a course would savour of *post hoc, ergo propter hoc.* The prosperity of the business is clearly due to its methods: an appreciation of these does not come within the scope of the present work. I do not think the managers of the firm would be so modest as to disclaim the credit due to them in view of the success of the firm; it is probable that the Works would have succeeded very well without any prosperity-sharing. Indeed, it is only because they were growing so fast at Warrington that they were removed to Port Sunlight.

Nobody will deny, however, even if the opinion of the managers themselves be not accepted, that the Port Sunlight scheme must powerfully influence the quality and the quantity of the products. To establish friendly relations is already a great step. The modern chaos of industrialism shows us the master pitted against the man, the former trying to obtain from the worker a maximum amount of labour for a minimum amount of pay, the latter resolved to obtain a maximum amount of pay for a minimum amount of labour. It shows us the worker ever ready to strike so as to obtain enhanced wages by force, the master willing to employ the blackleg and to starve his men into submission. Can such a state of things tend towards a large and a sound production? It cannot do so, for men are sensitive machines, and will neither produce their best work under compulsion, nor will they be able to do so when conditions are at their worst. Ability and willingness, therein lies the test, and the managers of Port Sunlight claim that the scheme has fostered both; if any one should speak with authority they should.

As regards ability they state that, their men being well fed, well housed, and cheerful, are able to produce more in their forty-eight hour week than their fellows who work longer hours under bad conditions. Evidence certainly goes to show that this is true, for there is a great deal of slacking in factories where the hours are long. At Port Sunlight the hours are short but well filled, so that the worker is not demoralized; nothing is so bad for him as reduced efficiency, for his mental as well as his physical muscles grow soft. Besides, there is the question of health. With the best of intentions the ill-fed and weakly man will never turn out as much, let alone as good, work as if he were strong and cheerful. Capacity is one thing but willingness is another. Employees are too often inclined to do a minimum of work or to "scamp" it as much as they dare. In an ideal factory, where the worker enjoys ideal conditions, his point of view changes. In the first place, owing to the fact that an appeal is made, not to his worst but to his best side, his conscience is aroused; he feels he must do as much and as good work as possible. At any rate, this is the experience of the managers at Port Sunlight, who state that the output and the quality per man have risen considerably during the last twenty years. They go so far as to say that in this increase they find a more than adequate return for the annual cost of the scheme. Apart, besides, from the awakened conscience of the worker there is a material influence which must not be underrated: the peculiar value of the post itself. The Sunlighter has more to lose than the ordinary worker; both have at stake their visible means of sustenance, but, whereas a change of employment may not mean very much for the ordinary worker, for the Sunlighter it means giving up his cottage and all that goes with it. This cruder side of the question must not be ignored, for the factory worker feels very clearly that he must justify short hours and good conditions by good work.

If we pass from the general to the particular, it is also clear that the men must be influenced by the knowledge that prosperity-sharing depends on there being prosperity to share. Thus, over and above the fear of losing at once both employment and citizenship of the Village, the worker feels that the continuance of benefits depends on the continuance of profits, and puts forth his best efforts. As he is working no longer for himself but for the good of the community to which he belongs he is thus gaining something as valuable as a happy home: an education in solidarity, in the knowledge that individual effort makes for the common good, an education in fraternity.

I was informed that the scheme had had most influence not so much on the quantity as on the quality of the products. However efficient the management may be it cannot be everywhere. The divisional manager must rely on his foremen and they on their subordinates; every man has something to do which it lies with him to do well enough to retain his billet or so very much better as to increase profits. If friendly feeling is engendered in the worker he naturally does his best, and it is this minute difference between good and very good which justifies the scheme in the eyes of its managers. Briefly, Port Sunlight is like a boat's crew, and it aims at encouraging the rowers to pull as hard as they can and all together. I was informed that the individual efficiency of the men has reacted to a remarkable degree upon the quality of the products, for they have become anxious to eliminate impurities. In a word, the firm states that any reputation it may have is a reputation for uniformity of product due almost entirely to the fact that the men will not allow flaws to mar their work. I have these facts direct, and they are worthy of credence, for it would be absurd to suggest that a limited liability company would continue such a scheme after twenty years' experience unless its directors had good reason to think that it paid.

It is of the utmost importance that the Port Sunlight scheme should pay, apart from its value to its own workers. If it were run at a loss, and the workers were conscious of the fact, they would be accepting doles and would become demoralized, but it is not easy to understand the economics of Port Sunlight, and there might be a loss without the workers knowing it, in which case they would benefit in health and education and yet retain their moral independence. The importance of our realizing that Port Sunlight is a paying venture lies in its value as an example to the industrial world. A certain number of manufacturers have already begun to see that it is to their advantage to improve in various ways the conditions of their employees; in England we must note such firms as Messrs. Cadbury, Rowntree, Armstrong, Whitworth & Co., Brunner, Mond & Co., Clarke, Nickolls & Coombs (Clarnico), etc.; on the Continent, and especially in America, these examples are far more numerous. Mr. Budgett Meakin quoted no less than two hundred and fifty instances of important firms where the conditions had deliberately been improved.

The importance of this question appears when we consider what prospects there are of other manufacturers coming into line with these progressive firms; these examples are precious, and the enormous development of such undertakings as the above clearly shows that good treatment of the men and good business often go together. If, little by little, similar schemes and minor improvements are everywhere introduced and react as favourably upon profits as they appear to have done at Port Sunlight, then there is hope for industrial England. A firm conviction on the part of the manufacturers that good treatment pays would effect a revolution which many years of factory legislation would fail to bring about. If we must appeal to the love of gain, then let us do so, for the first of our needs is to save the people, "to Christianize, socialize, industry," and we cannot afford to be particular as to the means to such an end.

If we consider the profits of Messrs. Lever Brothers and the success of other firms that have done something for the workers, we are driven to the hopeful conclusion that the new theory, "Humanity is the best policy," has begun to justify itself. As knowledge of the ventures spreads, of which Port Sunlight is so remarkable an instance, there is every reason to think that other manufacturers will be induced to join in the progressive movement, if only in their own interest. Thus, at last, we will be in a position to foresee the dawn of a new era, where man's inhumanity to man will be a decreasing quantity and commercial success will be commensurate with the kindly feeling upon which it rests.

Such as it is, however, paying as it probably is also, Port Sunlight is not a constituted body; it should not be forgotten that the will that ushered the Village into life can at a moment's notice thrust it back into nothingness. It is certain that, so long as Mr. W. H. Lever lives, the Village will continue, but surely such an institution as Port Sunlight should look forward to a longer life than that of a man. Indeed, if such a calamity as a large increase in rents were to befall the Village, say an average of three to four shillings, which would not compensate the firm for the prosperity-sharing contribution, the social results would be very grave. True, a generation or two would have been deeply influenced and several thousands of children would have been ideally fitted for the business of life, but, on the other hand, if the scheme were destroyed it would mean that it had failed commercially. If this were to happen the more generous development of commercialism would be checked and Port Sunlight would be added to the various phalansteries as an object lesson to the ardent. This peril is remote, but it is important to inquire what steps have been taken to cope with it. The answer is brief: no steps have or will be taken; the scheme must fend for itself. The position was concisely stated to me by Mr. Lever himself in the following terms:—

"My intentions for the future are quite precise. I feel that the position is: either the scheme pays the shareholders or it does not. If it does and my successors are convinced that it does, then it will be continued on the same lines as at present; if, however, invested as they will be with authority and responsibility, and enjoying full knowledge of conditions, they find that the scheme does not pay, then it will disappear. Everything is to remain *in situ*, and Port Sunlight must live on its merits or die. I do not think it would be a good thing to establish it on a trust basis. If the village, as it stands, and its precedential subsidy were made over to trustees, the latter, whether they were employers or employees, would be bound by the provisions of the trust. Thus, for contact between employer and employee, would be substituted contact between employer-trustee and employee-trustee, which is a very different and less valuable thing. Moreover, if we were to constitute Port Sunlight into a trust, definite conditions of subsidy would have to be laid down, so that we should have a fixed basis and varying conditions. We might have permanent benefits to the men and dwindling trade returns; in brief we should have prosperity-sharing and no adversity-sharing."

The foregoing states the case clearly from the

employer's point of view, and it is difficult to take exception to it if we remember that Port Sunlight is a commercial and not a philanthropic undertaking—if, especially, we admit that its chief value lies in its commercial character. In fact, given that the spirit of the above statement animates the management, it becomes all the more certain that the Village has already justified its existence, so that it has every reasonable chance of surviving as long as the Works themselves. The question of putting the scheme on a trust basis is more debatable. This has been done at Bournville, but it must be remembered that the two schemes are not comparable, and that there is, at Bournville, no definite industrial connection liable to be destroyed. It would seem very difficult to adjust the commercial principle of Port Sunlight with that of a trust deed, because the subsidy would have to be a fixed quantity. It would be quite impossible to empower the trustees to control (say) 10 per cent. of the net profits of Messrs. Lever Brothers: the Village does not need £40,000 a year any more than it can manage with £20,000; it must have £25,000 every year, neither more nor less. If the subsidy were to fluctuate, then rents would have to vary proportionately, and all the old evils of irregular bonuses which have already been fully dealt with would come to the fore. If, on the other hand, the subsidy were to be fixed at (say) £25,000 a year, nothing tells us that after a few years the sum would not prove either inadequate or too large. Then, if it were inadequate, rents would have to be raised, and the usefulness of the Village destroyed, in so far as it could then no longer house the poorer worker—or rents would go down so much that the employee's zeal would no longer be stimulated, and the commercial character of the scheme would vanish. It is, therefore, clear that things must remain as they are; but there does not seem to be much reason to fear that a scheme, the growth of which has concurred so remarkably with that of the business, will be allowed to lapse. In fact, we can assume that Port Sunlight is permanent, and that it will indefinitely pursue its beneficent career.

Apart from its future, and generally excellent in its intentions as it is, the Port Sunlight scheme is open to a few broad criticisms. One is the insecurity of tenure of the cottages, but it has already been explained that it is impossible to allow men to remain in the Village after they have left the Works, for there are only 720 houses, and more than double that number would be needed to house all the workers. General insecurity goes with all industrial employment, and it is really one of the most painful features of a workman's existence; since, however, many of the working classes lead somewhat wandering lives and continually remove,* this particular insecurity does not add very much to their problems. Besides, a good worker or a skilled artisan employed at the Works generally feels that his billet is almost secure, at any rate, as secure as in any other firm, so that his citizenship is also practically safe.

A more difficult question is that of the outlivers, of whom there are some two thousand odd. Among them are a number of single men and young girls,

* In the London County Council dwellings, in 1905-6, removals amounted to no less than 27 per cent. of the total number of tenancies; 30 and 40 per cent. are common rates.

most of whom find it either cheaper or pleasanter to live outside the Village, for it will be recalled that the conditions are there attractive mainly for the family. Many, however, must live outside the Village, because there are not houses enough to go round. If building operations are extended this difficulty will be minimized, but it is not likely to disappear, so that there will always be a section of the workers who do not benefit by Port Sunlight conditions. There exists in this regard a regrettable inequality which could only be redressed by calculating the individual value of prosperity-sharing for every employee, and giving him the option between a cash payment and residence in the Village. However, I believe that a family can always, by putting its name down, obtain a cottage after a reasonable time, and it is perhaps good that the applicant should prove himself in earnest before being admitted as a resident.

Apart from families, however, the single men and girls have some cause to complain, and it is to be hoped that the balance will ultimately be redressed. The best way would, of course, be to increase the number of houses, and to establish hostels on improved lines. There is also the point of view of the thrifty worker whose circumstances are such that he would rather draw cash bonuses than live in the Village. The strictures made on profit-sharing do not apply to the steady man; for him it is an ideal system. If he be single or have no children, or if he has relatives living in the neighbourhood with whom he could join forces, etc., he might prefer to live outside the Village and draw a cash equivalent. However, it is difficult to establish a test of thrift; the only way would be to give him shares in the undertaking, and they are not always obtainable at par. It is not easy to adjust such a large scheme as Port Sunlight to the needs of all the participants; in so far as its size allows, it is just and generally satisfactory.

The rock upon which Port Sunlight might split does not loom very large on the horizon; I mean paternalism—a danger which is always to be feared by social schemes conceived and conducted by a man or a very small group. It could nullify everything that is good in the idea, indeed, make it a social plague spot in a democratic country. The most eloquent testimony to the dangers of paternalism can be found in a novel—Mr. Harold Frederic's "Gloria Mundi"—which is singularly convincing. There, as in Port Sunlight, we find a man, or rather a family, animated with good intentions, convinced that it is their duty to do the best for those whose energies they direct, ministering to their wants, organizing their pleasures, attempting to raise and to moralize them, but succeeding only in sapping their vigour. Glorified pauperism is the end of many generous schemes; Port Sunlight is exposed to the danger, but it is likely to escape it. The fact that the controllers of the destinies of the Village do not sit *ex officio*, or otherwise, on the committees of the institutions, means that the pleasures of the people are free; besides, the principle of the scheme itself being purely commercial and non-philanthropic, there is little reason to fear that the villagers will at any time be coddled.

There is room, however, at Port Sunlight not only for minor alterations such as those which affect the liquor traffic, Sunday games and labour, extended restaurant facilities for the men, etc., but for a somewhat larger scheme. It is quite clear that absolute democracy cannot reign in the Village so long as the financial basis of the scheme remains unaltered; thus, the directors, Messrs. Lever Brothers, must retain absolute control over local conditions. Without, however, adopting another system, it appears possible to give the people a greater voice in the management of the estate. Already they can make their voice heard on general matters through their urban district council, but even there they are in a minority, and, moreover, this power is but a small matter in a district where conditions are so good as to make official interference unnecessary; the more important questions of rents and regulations do not come within the province of local authorities. At present the tenants can do no more than make individual protests and suggestions to the estate manager; they have, as a rule, but little to complain of, yet it would be a good thing to associate them more intimately with the fortunes of the estate they inhabit. This is the lesson of democracy all the world over. However unintelligent or even unjust the legislation may be that proceeds in the early days from democratic institutions, the value of the training received by the electors is an enormous national asset. I would therefore suggest for Port Sunlight a "Village Council." This body has been tried, and it originally controlled the institutions; when the latter became independent it died of inanition. There is room, however, for a purely advisory council, and it would have to ascertain from within the Villagers' opinion as regards rents, repairs, public gardens, open spaces, necessary and unnecessary institutions, Sunday closing, the drink traffic, etc. It could report on these subjects to the management and make recommendations which would carry more weight than isolated protests. If constituted on a democratic basis, *i.e.* if its members were elected by adult male and female suffrage, it could take an important part in moulding the destinies of the Village. It would never be incumbent on the management to give effect to its recommendations, but, at any rate, public opinion would be consulted and a buffer established between discontent, which may be unjustified, and officials who may be unsympathetic. Besides, it could be made into a useful institution of a more general nature than those at present existing. At Bournville it arranges for the co-operative purchase of seeds, tools, manure, etc.; this would best be done otherwise at Port Sunlight, but the Village Council might prove a valuable instrument of democratic education by quickening local interest in politics, arranging lectures, debates, etc. It would also add to the dignity of the scheme and establish yet more intimately the contact between employers and employees.

With these minor shortcomings and desiderata closes that which has been for me a fascinating study. I am not afraid of sounding a note of caution and of suggesting certain alterations, for I readily confess myself an enthusiast of the Port Sunlight idea and of all that it has brought into being. There is every reason to think that any changes that may take place, now that the Village bids fair to pay its way, will be in the direction of freedom—that the people will become at once both happier and better, and that the evolution so well begun will work towards beneficent ends. Thus the founder of the Village may well rejoice in his work and pride himself on a practical achievement unequalled in the annals of industrial Utopias.

INDEX

A

B

C

D

E

F

G

H

K

L

M

N

O

P

R

S

W

THE END

PRINTED BY WILLIAM CLOWES AND SONS, LIMITED, LONDON AND BECCLES.

A

Complete Catalogue

of the publications of

Alston Rivers, Ltd.

Chatterton House,
Brooke Street,
Holborn Bars,
London, E.C.

1 9

0 4

THE SQUARE MILE.

HORACE W. C. NEWTE.

Author of 'The Wife' and 'The Master Beast.' *6s.*

As author of "The Wife," Mr. Horace Newte has already considerable pretension to a leading place as a writer on "suburbia" Though he knows, and what is more can depict, the middle-class life as well as did George Gissing himself, he is never gloomy and there is always hope of his characters emerging from their troubles. His new book, he tells us, is concerned with quite commonplace people, but it is a charming story in which the author's genial humour is never lacking.

Novels published during the Spring and Summer, 1908.

HEATHER.

JOHN TREVENA.

Author of 'Furze the Cruel,' 'A Pixy in Petticoats,' 'Arminel of the West.' Third impression. *6s.*

The SUNDAY TIMES says:—"I have no hesitation in reckoning him one of the most original of our younger novelists. As a descriptive writer he can challenge comparisons with Mr. Phillpotts and beat him."

LEAVEN: A BLACK AND WHITE STORY.

DOUGLAS BLACKBURN.

Author of 'Prinsloo of Prinsloosdorp,' 'A Burgher Quixote,' etc. *6s.*

The ACADEMY says:—"Mr. Douglas Blackburn is in the happy position of realising that he has given us the very best novel on South Africa that has yet appeared. 'Leaven' is a magnificent story, written with a sense of humour combined with a sense of honour."

THE SWORD DECIDES!

MARJORIE BOWEN.

Author of 'The Viper of Milan' and 'The Glen o' Weeping.' Third impression. *6s.*

"This remarkable book is a series of the most vivid Italian illuminations, a collection of word pictures, as detailed and as splendid as the choicest gems from 'Les très riches heures' . . . She has told it with so much power and insight that it lives and convinces the reader without any need of proof. In this third novel the writer has gone back to the source of her first success, 'The Viper of Milan,' but she brings to this later story so much more strength of characterisation, so much greater freedom in the handling of the plot, and such a great deepening of emotional power, that the earlier book, praised as it was when it appeared, will seem a pale and amateurish novel beside its wonderful successor."—THE WESTMINSTER GAZETTE.

Novels published previous to 1908.

THE GLEN O' WEEPING.

MARJORIE BOWEN.

Author of 'The Sword Decides!' and 'The Viper of Milan.' Third Impression. 6*s*.

"The only thing to be said about 'The Viper of Milan' and its brilliantly successful successor, 'The Glen o' Weeping,' is that they carry one completely away. There is, in this second novel, every fine quality of its predecessor. . . It is an entire and complete success."—MORNING LEADER.

THE VIPER OF MILAN.

MARJORIE BOWEN.

Author of 'The Glen o' Weeping' and 'The Sword Decides!' Twelfth Impression. 6*s*.

"Miss Bowen is to be congratulated upon entering the ranks of our fictionists with so strong a piece of work; a story for which a wide popularity may confidently be predicted."—TELEGRAPH.

EXTON MANOR.

ARCHIBALD MARSHALL.

Author of 'The House of Merrilees,' etc. Fourth Impression. 6*s*.

"By far the best thing he has done. A novel which is not merely entertaining, but sane, wholesome and excellently observed—qualities by no means invariably found combined in modern fiction."—PUNCH.

PRIVY SEAL.

FORD MADOX HUEFFER.

Author of 'The Fifth Queen,' etc. 6*s*.

"'Privy Seal' is written with the same happy valiancy of language which made 'The Fifth Queen' so admirable, and the plan of the book is masterly. If you do not read Mr. Hueffer's book you will miss a rare enjoyment."—EVENING NEWS.

WORLD WITHOUT END.

WINIFRED GRAHAM

Author of 'Ezra the Mormon,' etc. 6*s*.

"One of those books that haunt! 'World Without End' has already attracted interest in high places. The incursion of an intrepid Englishman into the forbidden Shrine of Mashad is one of the most amazing tales which a novelist has had to tell. The Eastern scenes are altogether admirable. 'World Without End' is the author's best work."—WORLD.

MR. MEYER'S PUPIL.

EVA LATHBURY.

Author of 'The People Downstairs.' Second Impression. *6s.*

"The excessively charming lady who is pictured on the frontispiece and coloured wrapper of Miss Lathbury's novel, turns out to be as attractive in mind as she is in feature when we come to make her acquaintance through the pages of her diary. . . 'Mr Meyer's Pupil' is as clever and brightly written a story as we have read for a long time "—DAILY MAIL.

THE ADVENTURES OF COUNT O'CONNOR.

HENRY STACE.

Author of 'A Case for Compromise.' *6s.*

"Mr. Stace has really got the methods of the old masters to perfection. He will tell you the most astounding things about his hero in the dominions of the Great Mogul, with a grave expression which hitherto you had believed was inimitable."—THE STANDARD.

THE LORD OF LATIMER STREET.

JANE WARDLE.

Author of 'The Artistic Temperament.' *6s.*

"We venture to amplify our first prophecy, and say further, that if Miss Wardle is not a good deal heard of in connection with this book she will not get her deserts."—DAILY MAIL.

THE MEDDLER.

H. DE VERE STACPOOLE & W. A. BRYCE.

Author of 'The Blue Lagoon,' etc. *With eight illustrations and frontispiece. 6s.*

"Only people absolutely devoid of the sense of humour will fail to appreciate a book which forms as clever and original a contribution to the merry-makers' library as has been made for many a long day."—SCOTSMAN.

A BUNCH OF BLUE RIBBONS.

GEORGE MORLEY.

Author of 'Sweet Arden,' etc. *6s.*

"Mr. George Morley has long since established a lasting claim upon all who are lovers of, or dwellers in, Warwickshire."—BIRMINGHAM DAILY MAIL.

"It is probably safe to say that no other writer could have charged a story so full of the authentic and recognisable atmosphere of Warwickshire village life."—BIRMINGHAM DAILY POST.

AS DUST IN THE BALANCE.

MRS. H. H. PENROSE.

Author of 'The Unequal Yoke.' *6s.*

"Her work is a hundred times more genuine, more moving, stronger than most of that which wins a ready hearing. 'As Dust in the Balance' is a novel remarkable no less for finish than for strength."—MORNING LEADER.

THE UNEQUAL YOKE.

MRS. H. H. PENROSE.

Author of 'As Dust in the Balance.' *6s.*

"Mrs. H. H. Penrose, who is one of the women novelists to be taken into serious account, has not written anything better worth reading than 'The Unequal Yoke.' . . . Mrs. Penrose is a bold thinker and a strong writer."—WORLD.

THE TOWER OF SILOAM.

MRS. HENRY GRAHAM.

Author of 'The Disinherited of the Earth.' *6s.*

"This extremely readable and well-contrived novel should secure for its authoress a recognised position amongst the pleasantest of our writers of light fiction."—DAILY TELEGRAPH.

IN DESERT KEEPING.

EDMUND MITCHELL. *6s.*

"A sincere and successful novel."—TIMES.

"Full of exciting incident, but the fine character drawing saves it from the charge of sensationalism."—GLASGOW HERALD.

PEACE ON EARTH.

REGINALD TURNER. *6s.*

"The thorough originality, both in plot and treatment, of Mr. Turner's novel is its principal merit. . . . A thoroughly fresh piece of work and a novel of marked power. It gives Mr. Turner a firm position."—VANITY FAIR.

THE COUNTERMINE.

ARTHUR WENLOCK.

Author of 'As Down of Thistle.' *6s.*

"Surely few more commendatory things can be said of any novel that may be fairly said of this one—that it makes you read whether you will or no."—SCOTSMAN.

A CAPTAIN OF MEN.

E. ANSON MORE. *6s*

"The story is exceedingly well written, and the characters are worked out with consummate skill. The style of the book makes it doubly interesting and enjoyable."—DUNDEE COURIER.

General Literature,

Autumn MCMVIII.

PROPHETS, PRIESTS AND KINGS.

A. G. GARDINER.

With over 40 portraits. *7s. 6d. net.*

A series of character sketches entirely devoted to distinguished persons of every profession and station, commencing with the Kaiser and concluding with King Edward, the one exception to the rule that only the living are criticised being the late Sir Henry Campbell-Bannerman, whose death occurred so recently that the collection would certainly not be complete without his highly revered name.

WATER: ITS ORIGIN AND USE.

W. COLES-FINCH.

By W. Coles-Finch, Resident Engineer to the Brompton, Chatham Gillingham and Rochester Water Company With over 150 illustrations. Demy 8vo. *21s. net.*

Mr. Coles-Finch's book should prove to be the standard popular work on the element with which it deals. Though written by an expert, "Water: Its Origin and Use," is not a purely scientific book; it is, as the author remarks in his preface, "simply an ordinary person's interpretation of what he sees in Nature and represents his best efforts to describe the same."

How successful have been these efforts is attested by the warm eulogies of many eminent scientists to whom advance copies have been submitted.

An attractive volume, embellished by many beautiful illustrations, including Alpine scenes from photographs taken by Mrs. Aubrey le Blond, who has achieved wide renown in this branch of art.

PSYCHE.

LOUIS COUPERUS.

With twelve illustrations by Dion Clayton Calthrop. *3s. 6d.*

"Is fit to place on the shelf beside the fairy tales of Hans Andersen. It is more serious, but it ought to appeal to everybody who can appreciate a tale like that of 'The Little Mermaid.'"—BIRMINGHAM POST.

BABEL.

LOUIS COUPERUS.

Illustrated. *3s. 6d.*

In "Babel" the author has woven a romance around the worship of Baal and the builders of the great tower.

General Literature published previous to the Autumn of 1908.

THE CONTEMPORARY POETS SERIES.

PAPER COVERS, Imp. 16mo. 1s. net per volume.

This Series comprises the following nine volumes,—"London Dead," C. K. Burrow; "Lost Water," Mrs. I. K. Lloyd; "A Ballad of Victory," Mrs. D. Radford; "The Soul's Destroyer," W. H. Davies (Second Edition); "From Inland," F. M. Hueffer; "Repose," J. Marjoram; "Sealed Orders," W. H. Pollock; and "Democratic Sonnets," W. M. Rossetti (two volumes).

WITH THE M.C.C. IN AUSTRALIA.

MAJOR PHILIP TREVOR. *1s. net.*

"Contains full records of the tour, given with the author's customary frankness, fairness, and good sense."—THE GLOBE.

FROM A HERTFORDSHIRE COTTAGE.

W. BEACH THOMAS.

With frontispiece. 3s. 6*d*.

"We take leave to bring the book to the notice of our readers as one of the best, as it is one of the least pretending, that has emanated from a country cottage for some years."—COUNTRY GENTLEMAN.

THE SPIRIT OF PARLIAMENT.

DUNCAN SCHWANN, M.P. 3*s*. 6*d*. *net*

"He has literary grace and charm; he thinks; he is an idealist; he is a choice scholar; and he has a saving grace of humour."—MANCHESTER CITY NEWS.

THE SEARCH FOR THE WESTERN SEA.

LAWRENCE J. BURPEE.

Public Librarian at Ottawa. *With over 50 illustrations and maps.* 16*s. net.*

"The illustrations are good, so also the maps, the index, and the valuable bibliography of works dealing with the exploration of N.W. America—altogether the book is a model."—PUBLISHER'S CIRCULAR.

TO-DAY IN GREATER BRITAIN.

THE CITIZEN BOOKS.

Edited by W. Beach Thomas. 1*s. net.*

"This is the first of a series intended to be 'guide books to the present.' A very useful and instructive new departure in educational literature."—OUTLOOK.

THE FACE OF ENGLAND.

THE CITIZEN BOOKS.

A. K. Collett. Edited by W. Beach Thomas. 1*s. net.*

"He would be an ungrateful youngster who would not thank Mr. A. K. Collett for a book of geography free from long lists of names, facts, and figures."—PALL MALL GAZETTE.

THE NEW TRANSVAAL.

MISS M. C. BRUCE.

Cloth 1*s.* 6*d. net. Paper* 1*s. net.*

"One of the best books on South Africa we have had for a long time. It is priced at a shilling only, but it has more stuffing in it than half the pretentious expensive books which have been manufactured about the sub-Continent. The authoress is one who knows. That is apparent on every page. The book is full of common sense . . . we congratulate Miss Bruce on her clever work."—SOUTH AFRICA.

FRANCE IN THE 20TH CENTURY.

W. L. GEORGE.

Author of 'Labour and Housing at Port Sunlight.' 6*s. net.*

"This book 'lets in fresh air,' and wil doubtless tend to sweeten the imagination of its readers, and lead them even further into the flowery closes of the Entente Cordiale."—DAILY TELEGRAPH.

FAUST.

GOETHE.

Translated in Verse by Sir George Buchanan, C.B., K C.V.O. *Leathe* 3*s*. 6*d*. *net*. *Buckram*, 2*s*. 6*d*. *net*.

"The work of a scholar who has caught the true spirit of the original, and is able to interpret it to English readers in metre which is elegant correct, and sonorous."—MORNING POST.

THE BOOK OF LIVING POETS.

Edited by Walter Jerrold. 7*s*. 6*d*. *net*.

"An excellent anthology. Chosen entirely from the work of living poets, it will bear comparison in interest and beauty with anthologies of a far wider scope. Within its four hundred pages some fifty or sixty men and women deal with many aspects of modern life, or with thoughts or emotions rising out of it."—MORNING POST.

THE SPIRIT OF THE PEOPLE.

FORD MADOX HUEFFER.

Author of 'The Soul of London,' etc. 5*s*. *net*.

"A pleasant book for a reader of cultured tastes; it reflects a genial temperament behind a not uncritical eye, and it is written in a facile style that presents the idea in the fewest words and with the least effort."—SCOTSMAN.

THE SOUL OF LONDON.

FORD MADOX HUEFFER.

Author of 'Privy Seal, etc., etc. 5*s*. *net*.

"Many readers will, we are convinced, look at their London with clearer eyes and better understanding after a perusal of this remarkable book."—DAILY TELEGRAPH.

THE HEART OF THE COUNTRY.

FORD MADOX HUEFFER.

Author of 'The Fifth Queen,' etc. etc. 5*s*. *net*.

"We have had 'country' books of the most varied character, from that of Gilbert White to those of Richard Jefferies, but Mr. Hueffer has taken a new and interesting line of his own, and his really beautiful work will, assuredly, make him many friends."—DAILY TELEGRAPH.

FURTHER INDIA.

HUGH CLIFFORD, C.M.G.

"Another volume in this most excellent series. Mr. Clifford has produced a thoroughly readable, trustworthy and fascinating book, well indexed and well illustrated."—THE ACADEMY.

ST. LAWRENCE BASIN AND ITS BORDERLANDS.

S. E. DAWSON, Litt.D., F.R.S.C.

"He is writing a geographical rather than a political history, and, incidentally, demonstrates how interesting that can be made."—THE STANDARD.

THE NILE QUEST.

SIR HARRY JOHNSTON, G.C.M.G., K.C.B.

"The record of the quest could not fail to be a fascinating story. Sir Harry Johnston has done a useful service in setting forth the often tangled results of African exploration in a clear narrative."—THE SPECTATOR.

TIBET THE MYSTERIOUS.

COL. SIR THOS. HOLDICH, K.C.M.G., K.C.I.E., C.B.

"It is a story full of notable and romantic episodes, and it is brilliantly narrated by Sir Thomas Holdich, who gives, moreover, graphic descriptions of the country itself and its people. No more fascinating book on Tibet has appeared."—TRUTH.

Further Volumes in this important series will be announced from time to time. . . . .

Spotted something that isn't quite right?

Let us know and we'll fix it for future reprints.
And as a thank you for your diligence, we'll
send you a free Sothis book of your choice.

publisher@sothis.press

This page intentionally left blank

Made in the USA
Monee, IL
09 November 2026

68245473R10215